In Their F

Exploring a Northern .

Jane Coll

Published in 2022 by Kindle Direct Publishing

© Jane Coll 2022

ISBN 9798842554935

The cover is illustrated by Stuart Mingham, who also designed the Northern Pilgrims' Way guidebook and various of their information panels. The central mountain is Morven, the highest peak in Caithness, and various other features in the area are incorporated into the design. Note the shadows of past pilgrims! To see more of Stuart's work, go to:
www.art-from-viewpoints.co.uk.

Acknowledgements

Thanks must first go to Deacon John Woodside who's own book inspired this one and then to Barbara and John of the St Anne's Book Club, Thurso for their work on the saints of the area that became the Northern Saints Trails. Thanks also to those who formed the Northern Pilgrims Way Group SCIO, taking the project to a wider audience – Karl, Alison, Philip, Marilyn, Nick, Margaret.

I am grateful to Garry Robertson for the loan of some invaluable books, without which this would have been a very slim volume. Audrey Munro sent me material from her collection of the works of the Rev Dr Archibald B Scott B.D., a Church of Scotland minister based in Helmsdale in the early 1900's who wrote extensively about the early church in this part of the world. His writing may become available through the Timespan Museum. For anyone interested in accessing this collection, please read my section 'Celtic saints in a world context' first! My last source was Roy McKenzie, who told me about 'super altars.'

Finally, I am grateful to a long-time friend, Ann Johnson, for reading over the first draft and suggesting various improvements.

'Let not many of you become teachers, my brethren, for you know that we who teach shall be judged with greater strictness. For we all make many mistakes.' (The Letter of James 3:1-2)

Contents

Abbreviations

CBP	Caithness Broch Project
CFC	Caithness Field Club
HER	Highland Historic Environment Record (https://her.highland.gov.uk)
JOGT	John O'Groats Trail
NPW	Northern Pilgrims' Way
NST	Northern Saints Trails

Eccl Hist is *Ecclesiastical History of Caithness and Annals of Caithness Parishes*;

Cat is *The History of the Province of Cat (Caithness and Sutherland), From the Earliest Times to the Year 1615*;

Inv is *Third Report and Inventory of Monuments and Constructions in the County of Caithness*.

Scott is the various articles by Rev Archibald B Scott B.D.

Watson is *The Celtic Place-Names of Scotland.*

Full details are in the Bibliography.

Biblical quotes are taken from the Revised Standard Version.

Introduction

To trace the history of the re-established medieval pilgrimage route between St Duthac's, Tain and St Magnus' Kirkwall, we have to go back to 2017 and St Anne's RC church hall in Thurso, where a small book club met to discuss Deacon John Woodside's book 'Together in Christ: Following the Northern Saints'. The group were surprised at the number of saints with connections to Caithness. A fairly light-hearted comment about the desirability of bringing these saints to the attention of those living in the county developed a life of its own and grew into a work that we think has answered Deacon Woodside's own wish, expressed in the final paragraph of his introduction;

> It is hoped that this short book will inspire you to do some saint researching of your own and discover the Christian genes that inform the history of several peoples who would eventually unite to become the Scottish Nation.[1]

During our researches, we added wishes of our own. In addition to the general aim of making the early Christian history of Caithness more widely appreciated, we were keen to remind the various Christian denominations of our common heritage in the hope of furthering the already positive ecumenical spirit in Caithness and the Highlands in general. At a more prosaic level, we wanted to persuade tourists to

---

1 J. Woodside, *Together in Christ: Following the Northern Saints*, p. 3.

spend some time in the area. We hoped that this project would give them a reason to pause and explore – we have far more to offer than beaches and cliffs, spectacular though these are!

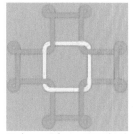
The NST logo was inspired by the carved cross known as the Skinnet Stone because it originally stood at the chapel and graveyard site at Skinnet, on the outskirts of the village of Halkirk (site no 38 on the NST). It is a Class II Pictish Symbol stone, dated to the 7th-9th century. The site can still be visited but the stone, now damaged, has been moved to the North Coast Visitor Centre, Thurso. Perhaps someday a replica will be made and placed on the original site.

The task of re-establishing the Tain-Kirkwall pilgrimage route had two distinct but overlapping phases, beginning with the research into the Caithness saints, resulting in the Northern Saints Trails of Caithness. Our first task was to find a structure through which to present this material. The most cursory of initial researches had shown that there was an embarrassment of material on the subject. Every corner of Caithness had its ruined chapels, holy wells and ancient graveyards. The list of saints with Caithness connections grew and grew. The dilemma was how to present this material in a logical manner. So we decided to construct several local circular routes. Then we realised that we could not limit this to Caithness, or even Caithness and North Sutherland.

How could you talk of Maelrubha's[2] connection to Farr without mentioning Applecross or Duthac's connection to Killimster Moss without mentioning Tain? So we decided to look at the North Highlands in fairly general terms and have more detailed routes based in Wick and Thurso.

For the Highland-wide route, we have followed the normal practice of moving in a clockwise direction. If you are not doing this, please adapt the information to your own plans.

Caithness also has a rich heritage of brochs and chambered cairns. It would be well worth the reader's time to check the various web pages giving details of these and include any that fall within easy reach of their chosen route. I have not included details of them in my descriptions, partly in the interests of clarity but also because this information is readily available from other sources.

During this research, the group realised that there was enough evidence still available on the medieval pilgrimage route between St Duthac's, Tain and St Magnus' Cathedral, Kirkwall to allow for a historically accurate re-establishment of this route. So began the second phase – developing the Northern Pilgrims' Way.

---

2 Pronunciation varies but is roughly a cross between 'Mulrua' and 'Moolrua'

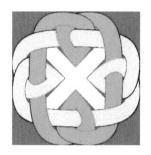 The logo for the Northern Pilgrims' Way took its inspiration from another important Class II Pictish Symbol stone, the Ulbster Stone. This originally stood in the graveyard of St Martin's Chapel, Ulbster (site no 20 on the NST). The pointed curves are an unusual feature of Celtic knotwork and are found on the Ulbster Stone. The two braids represent the two saints, Duthac and Magnus. By happy coincidence, the central shape forms the St Andrew's Cross, as featured on the Scottish flag.

As it is expected that most travellers will move from south to north, I have followed the route in this direction, describing the pilgrimage route and then the Caithness trails. I have not attempted a comprehensive history of either the places mentioned or the saints associated with them. Instead, I have focussed on those aspects of history and biography that are relevant to the Early and Medieval Church. The Bibliography will give ideas on where more detailed information can be found. Also, many communities on the NPW and relevant interest groups have websites with more specific, local information. Having said that, I hope that I have added enough detail to encourage you to explore the places that you will be travelling through and to feel a connection with those who have walked this Way before you.

In the interests of simplicity, I have not endlessly repeated the word 'saint' with the various names.

Please take it as read that, if a name is listed in the Alphabetical List of Saints, then that person is regarded as a saint. All but a few very obscure saint's names mentioned in the text are included in this list.

I have divided the material into four parts as follows;

- Part One discusses some relevant background topics

- Part Two gives information on the places that the NPW route passes through and ends with two poems, one from mainland Scotland and one from Orkney.

- Part Three gives some historical details to place the saints in context; some modern options for today's pilgrims and describes the Northern Saints trails (six circular routes within Caithness) with a few short notes on the non-Caithness sites that are on the NC500

- Part Four gives brief biographies of the saints mentioned in the previous parts; a calendar of these saints feast days and the bibliography.

PART ONE: Some background

'Now his parents went to Jerusalem every year at the feast of the Passover. And when he was twelve years old, they went up according to custom.' (Luke 2:41-42)

What is a pilgrimage?

The standard dictionary definition of the word 'pilgrimage' is 'journey to a holy place; the journey of life' and of a pilgrim as 'a traveller, esp. one who journeys to visit a holy place as an act of devotion; a wanderer'[3] This urge to endow places with spiritual/religious significance and to attach 'added value' to journeys to them seems to be universal. Sometimes the place becomes a pilgrimage site because of its associations with specific religious leaders – think Jerusalem and Mecca. In other cultures, more emphasis is placed on the natural features of sites that encourage a sense of the supernatural – think Ayers Rock in Australia. On a smaller scale, there are sacred trees, holy wells and revered burial grounds on every continent.

For many centuries, the word 'pilgrimage' was used simply to describe a journey to one of the main holy sites of the main religions. For Christianity, this meant Jerusalem and Rome for the majority of pilgrims. Other sites came and went in fame depending on the popularity of the saint linked to them or the miracles associated with them. Perhaps the most

---

[3] Collins New English Dictionary

enduring of these saintly sites is Santiago de Compostella in Spain, the resting place of the bones of St James the apostle. This has been a pilgrimage destination since the 9th century. In more modern times, the Marian sites of Fatima, Lourdes and Medjugorje draw many thousands of pilgrims every year. According to the United Nations, one in three travellers is a pilgrim (as stated in the Catholic Herald 2 Jan 2020).

At its peak in the 14th and 15th centuries, pilgrimage was a well-regulated activity. People went on pilgrimage voluntarily to pray for a cure for themselves or others; to give thanks for answered prayers; to expiate a crime or sin or simply to move closer to God. They could also be sent on pilgrimage as a punishment for wrong-doing of various kinds. An official pilgrim would wear a recognised costume that included a pilgrim token[4], staff and pouch. In gentler climates, a pilgrim hat with wide floppy brim was part of this outfit but I suspect that the winds in these northern parts made this impractical! Each item of this costume had a practical purpose – the token entitled the pilgrim to free overnight hospitality, usually at monasteries along the way but also at private homes; the staff had a metal hook at the end and could be used to keep the pouch dry while fording a river or to fend off wolves or bandits; the pouch held the day's food, probably a chunk of beremeal bannock and cheese for those travelling in the north of Scotland. The floppy hat, when worn, protected the face from the elements

---

[4] The NPW pilgrim token can be bought via their website.

and could have the pilgrim token pinned to its rim, providing easy identification of the traveller's pilgrim status.

Human nature being what it is, politics also played a part in some pilgrimages. Rulers would go on pilgrimage to Rome to demonstrate to the rest of the world that they were sufficiently secure in their position to be able to leave their kingdoms for several months without risk of a coup and wealthy enough to travel in style, giving alms to the poor on the way. They would meet up with other leaders and strengthen existing or create new trade agreements. Indeed, the practice of pilgrimage has been credited with the spread of cultural and scientific knowledge around Europe. One rather surprising ruler who falls into this group is the Scottish King Macbeth. Contrary to popular belief, he was a successful and long-lasting king, reigning from 1040 to 1057. According to the chronicler, Marianus Scotus, in his 'Chronicle of World History', Macbeth arrived in Rome in 1050 'scattering silver like seed to the poor in Rome'[5]

In our modern world, where organised religion is not the force that it used to be, people still feel the need to attribute significance to visiting specific places and the term 'pilgrimage' is broadening out to include any journey that has a specific spiritual purpose. This must be more than just a relaxing holiday or even a 'getting back to nature' exercise. It could be an afternoon's journey to visit the grave of a parent or other loved one, perhaps in an effort to heal

---

[5] See 'Macbeth:Man and Myth' p.78

a wound; to say something that should have been said while the person was alive. It could be a journey to a retreat centre to re-establish the practice of daily prayer. It could be an exercise in leaving behind modern life for a period in order to work out what one's priorities should be. A definition used by a Church of Scotland minister recently sums up this broader usage of the word:

> 'Pilgrimage is a journey where the destination is ultimately the same as that from which you set out. Through it, you are asking God to show you your life, your home, your place in a new light.'[6]

For those following a route such as the NPW, with its strong historical links, another definition sums up the motive for many walkers: 'They are reliving the past in order to live the future.'[7] For most of us, the word conjures up a picture of a long-distance walk to a specific place. Very often this will be a 'thin place' where the barrier between earth and heaven seems to be less than in other places. Science has yet to explain this phenomenon but those who have sensed it know that it is real.

The routes described in this book would also have been used by the early saints as they brought Christianity to the north of Scotland. They would typically have spent some time in a monastic setting or under the authority of a bishop before setting out on

---

[6] Rev Julia Meason, East Church, Kirkwall on 20th August 2021
[7] From a fellow-participant in the above event.

their travels. As a sign that they were authorised to preach the Gospel and say Mass, they would be given consecrated mini-altar stones with them, called 'super altars'. One such stone was found at Wick harbour during dredging operations in 1918. It is now in the National Museum of Scotland, where it has been dated as belonging to the 7th/8th century. [8]The stone is apr four inches square and one inch thick. It has a central cross and four smaller crosses at each corner. These could represent the five wounds of Christ on the cross or the larger cross could represent Christ and the smaller ones either the four gospels or the four corners of the world, symbolising Jesus' instruction to the apostles to 'make disciples of all nations' (Matt.28:19). The central cross is in the shape of what is known as the Jerusalem Cross. This is interesting, as the Jerusalem Cross is typically associated with the Crusades of the 11th and 12th centuries but must have been in common use long before then.

The Wick super-altar

---

[8] Details of the super-altars and the photo are from Roy MacKenzie.

What is a saint

In the first nine or ten centuries of the Church, all that was needed for someone to be declared a saint was his or her reputation as someone who had led a holy life. They may have had specific gifts of healing or preaching while alive and there would be evidence of miracles associated with their relics or burial places. In the time of St Duthac, this seems to have still been the accepted practice as there is no record of a formal canonisation process. Gradually, a more formal process developed. Partly due to his position as joint earl of Orkney, there is more detail available for the process of recognising Magnus as a saint, with the key features being the recognition of his death as martyrdom, the translation of his body to a specific shrine and the annual celebrations of this event. The most important feature for both saints was their reputation for holiness among the population.

The process of canonisation moved from public acclamation (St Duthac) to approval by the local bishop, who would look for evidence of martyrdom, miracles associated with prayers to the deceased and an incorrupt body. He would then signal the canonisation by organising the removal of the body to a church (St Magnus). By the time of Pope Alexander III (1159-81) most cases would be approved by the pope. This became mandatory under Gregory IX (1227-41). The process of canonisation for Magnus took over twenty years.[9] Linked to this process of canonisation

---

[9] See Mgt Buer Soiland PhD.pdf and
https://uhi.academia.edu/SarahJaneGibbon

was the organisation of the country into diocese with a bishop in charge of appointing local priests, organising church buildings, gathering tithes, setting up systems for the care of the traveller and the destitute and generally assisting the political leaders in maintaining order. This process occurred mainly in the 12th century, with Bishop Gilbert being responsible for organising Caithness and Sutherland. The bishop[10] would own land in his area and the revenues from this supported both the lives of himself and his priests and the charitable activities in the diocese. The Caithness bishop owned land at Scrabster, Lythmore, Dorrery and Durness. The place name 'Papigoe' at Wick may also indicate Church land. There are records of the Bishop of Orkney receiving tithes from Dunnet and Canisbay, suggesting ownership of land there. As life became more complicated, centralised and bureaucratic, the local bishop became more involved in secular matters – the bishop's palace was often the only centre of learning, of secure storage for important documents and even of secure accommodation for people awaiting trial.

While Gilbert was bishop of Caithness and Sutherland, he moved his cathedral to Dornoch, deeming it safer than either Thurso or Halkirk where previous bishops had been based.[11] The situation

---

10 A note on terminology: the literature sometimes refers to abbots where modern usage would refer to bishops. Similarly, priests may be referred to as monks even when they were not attached to a monastery.

[11] See the section 'Part Two: A Tale of Two Bishops' for reasons why Bishop Gilbert might not have felt safe in Caithness.

regarding what land belonged to whom was complicated by conflicting loyalties for the local earls, who owed allegiance to the Scottish king and/or the Norwegian one, depending on the state of the current power struggles. This topic is outwith the scope of my writings and all I can say is that, while Caithness and Sutherland have always been recognised as distinct land masses, they have been treated as one unit for ecclesiastical purposes.

With the Reformation in the mid-16th century, declaring people as saints was not accepted in the Reformed Churches, as only God knew who was or was not in Heaven. So only those named as saints in Scripture should be so called and the practice of venerating saints relics or burial places and of praying to them was wrong. Praying to saints was also wrong because it suggested that we needed intermediaries between us and God when in fact all we needed to do was speak directly to God.

The Roman Catholic Church continues the process of canonisation as it feels that it is good to have examples of lives of heroic virtue for us to emulate. Also 'We should show honour to the saints of God, as being members of Christ, the children and friends of God, and our intercessors.'[12] On the first objection, it replies that God gives us signs to help us to determine who should be declared a saint or not. On the second, it argues that 'We pray to the saints, … not that God may through them know our petitions, but that our

---

[12] Thomas Aquinas. *Summa Theologica.* Kindle edition, location 80340

prayers may be effective through their prayers and merits.'[13] The current process has the following main stages:[14]

1. The person must have had a reputation for holiness during their lifetime
2. This reputation must endure beyond their death, so the process of canonisation does not start until at least five years after their death
3. Someone appointed by the bishop of their diocese, known as a 'postulator', collects evidence of the person's virtues from people who knew them and from writings by or concerning them.
4. The bishop sends the results to Rome, where they are studied by a theological commission and by the Congregation for the Causes of Saints. If they decide that the case has merit and the Pope agrees, the person is granted the title of 'Venerable'.
5. Where the person has died a martyr's death, they are immediately given the title 'Blessed'. In other cases, there has to be evidence of a miracle occurring as a result of prayers to them after their death.
6. After evidence of another miracle, the Pope decides whether or not to declare the person a saint.

Once someone is declared a saint, they are allocated a feast day, either in the world-wide Calendar of Saints or in one specific to their region.

---

[13] Thomas Aquinas. *Summa Theologica.* Kindle edition, location 57539
[14] from an article by Joseph Pronechen in the National Catholic Register, found at https://www.ncregister.com/blog/how-does-a-person-become-a-saint

Celtic saints in a world context

The terms 'Celtic saints' and 'the Celtic Church' are surrounded by controversy, beginning with the pronunciation of the word 'Celtic'. Until recently, it was commonly pronounced as for the Glasgow football team of that name (so 'Seltic'). It is currently fashionable to pronounce it with a hard 'c', as in 'coal' (so 'Keltic). The academics will tell you that the hard 'c' is the correct version as the name goes back to the origins of the Celtic peoples who migrated across Europe from Central Asia Minor, whose language only used the hard 'c'. The debate can become very detailed! Here, I will comment only that, in Scotland in the 1870's a Roman Catholic Maris brother, Brother Walfrid, working in the city of Glasgow, decided to form a football team to keep the unemployed men out of trouble and to raise money for food for the poor. These men were of Irish or western-Highland families, so he decided to call his football team 'Celtic'. At this time, the term was being used for peoples from areas whose native language was a variant of Gaelic – North-West Scotland; Ireland; Wales; Brittany. Brother Walfred, aware of the academic argument for a hard 'c', tried to introduce this for the name of his team but the good people of Glasgow would have nothing to do with it – they had used a soft 'c' for generations and saw no need to change. I suspect, with no academic research whatsoever to back-up my idea, that the modern adoption of the hard 'c' has as much to do with people distancing themselves from the football team as it has to do with academic rigour. Fortunately, we do not need to worry about pronunciation in a written work and the reader is free to choose whatever version they wish.

The term 'Celtic Church' has another layer of meaning added to that of pronunciation – was it an independent body existing in the lands of the Celtic peoples or was it simply a local variant on the universal Christian Church whose headquarters were in Rome? This is a rather more important debate than that of pronunciation as it has affected, and continues to affect, how historians interpret past events. This in turn affects the public's perception of both historical events and modern society. The debate falls roughly into two periods – the couple of centuries following the Reformation and the last fifty years or so. I mention it here, not to be divisive but quite the opposite. One of the aims of the founder-members of the Northern Pilgrims' Way Group was to remind all Christian denominations of our shared heritage. These Celtic saints belong to all of us and the hope is that, by reminding everyone of this aspect of our history, we will provide a platform for joint prayer and reflection. The following arguments are presented here for those who might want to investigate the topic in more detail. It is perfectly possible to feel an empathy with 'our' saints and to retrace their footsteps without giving any thought at all to what larger grouping they were part of.

In the post-Reformation period, much local history was collected and written down by church ministers as they were some of the few with the education and time to devote to this. They did valuable work in preserving the history of their parishes. It was in their interests, quite possibly at a sub-conscious level, to portray the Celtic Church as a separate organisation to the Roman Catholic Church. They could thus claim to be returning to the true roots of Christianity rather than being a break-away organisation. There is no historical evidence to support this argument and all sorts of evidence to support the view that the Celtic Church was simply the Universal Church in the Celtic areas – basically the same organisation but with its own local variations. These local variations can be seen even in today's inter-connected world. This is not the place to go into the details of the historical evidence – I mention the debate simply to warn the reader that some of the works quoted or listed in the Bibliography need to be treated with caution when referring to church history. What modern academics accept was a natural evolution from more local to more universal practices, are described by some church historians as a power-grab by the foreign invaders, subjugating the defenceless local minority.

Recently, writers have returned to the topic of the Celtic Church. They tend to by-pass the arguments about church governance and concentrate instead on the idea of the Celtic peoples as being close to nature and aware of the presence of God in his creation. This fits in well with the modern concerns about global warming It has also drawn attention to the areas associated with the Celtic peoples, providing economic benefits in the shape of religious tourism. This was an aim of founder-members of the Northern

Pilgrims' Way Group – to provide a possible source of additional income for farmers/crofters/small businesses on the Way. However, I feel obliged to issue a warning – please do not put on rosy-tinted glasses when reading about the Celtic peoples! Some authors present them as having a child-like simplicity; isolated from the corrupting influences of the wider world, they found God in the goodness of his creation, praising him in poetry and song inspired by their surroundings rather than the formal liturgies of the Roman Church. While these modern writings can be beautiful and inspiring, they are rather misleading. Writing as someone who's faith comes directly from Columba and whose childhood was not all that far removed from the lifestyle of these Celtic peoples, I can confirm that this life was not some idyll, sheltered from the corrupting influences of more cynical peoples. We were good, bad and mixed, just like everyone else. Yes, we were very aware of God's creation but that is because our lives were governed by the elements and the seasons of the year. On specifically liturgical matters, you only have to look at the Book of Durrow or Kells to realise that the formal liturgy of the Celtic Church was just as elaborate as elsewhere in Christendom.

Modern academic thought on the subject can be summed up in the words of Proff Tom Clancy who concludes that the most accurate word to describe Christianity in Scotland in these early centuries is 'catholic' where the word means:

> … in broad conformity with the core beliefs, and general practices of the churches of early

medieval Europe, and possessed of theological sensibilities which we can see as part of an evolving continuum with those beliefs that crystallised into doctrine throughout Europe in the twelfth and thirteenth centuries.[15]

For anyone interested in following up this debate, see references to the writings of Ian Bradley, Donald Meek and Tom Clancy at the end of the Bibliography.

Finally, an explanation of why several of the biographies of the saints in Part Four say that the saint attended the Synod of Whitby and voted for or against the proposed changes. This was noteworthy because it is linked to the 'Celtic versus Rome' argument. Two points are worth noting – the issues discussed at the Synod and the fact that the voting did not go according to partisan lines. The Synod was called by the King of Northumbria in 664 in order to standardise various practices throughout the land. A debate had raged throughout Europe for some time about the correct date of Easter, with some areas using the Julian Calendar and others using the more modern and accurate Gregorian Calendar to calculate the date. This had practical problems for clergy travelling from one area to another. It also created problems for the laity, including the king – his branch of Christianity (Celtic) celebrated Easter according to different calculations from those used by his wife's (Roman) branch. The date of Easter also fixed the dates of the

[15] Proff T.O. Clancy 'Celtic or Catholic – Writing the history of Scottish Christianity, A.D. 664-1093' pub 2002 and available at https://archive.org

forty days of Lent that immediately precede Easter and it was the custom then for couples to abstain from marital relations during Lent. The King was having to abstain for his own forty days and for those of his wife. As they did not exactly overlap, he felt that he was having to overdo his penance. There were several other practices where some areas did one thing and other areas did another – the shape of the monk's tonsure being the best known. In the Celtic tradition, monks shaved their heads from ear to ear, leaving the crown and back alone. In the Roman tradition, monks shaved their heads over the crown, leaving a circle around the edges. The reason for these styles and why they differed has been lost in the mists of time and modern monks tend to just have an all-over shave once a month or so.[16]

These differences have been used to support the idea that the Celtic and Roman communities represented two different Churches. In fact, they simply represent the effect of increasing distance from the administrative centre. The Synod was not discussing the amalgamation of two previously independent bodies but the standardisation of some of their practices in order to facilitate co-operation both within Britain and between Britain and Europe. There were no theological issues at stake, nor was there any dispute about the hierarchy of the Church. Some representatives of the Celtic tradition supported changing to the Roman usages, others vehemently

---

[16] I recently read that the Celtic style represented slavery – the monk was the slave of God.

opposed any change – Adamnon, Abbot of Iona supported the changes but Colman, Abbot of Lindisfarne, resigned his position rather than accept them. The king himself eventually supported the Roman practices, as did a majority of the delegates.

One other interesting note is that the religious community at Whitby consisted of both monks and nuns. The most senior figure in 664 was Abbes Hilda, who hosted the Synod.

By the time of Duthac and Magnus, the ecclesiastical pattern in the north of Scotland was moving from missionaries centred round a monastery to diocese in charge of a bishop, with his cathedral and various outlying churches. This arrangement had the advantage of being cheaper to administer than the Benedictine-style enclosed monasteries. Local political leaders, or sometimes the king himself, would grant the bishop lands and the revenues from this would support the bishop's work. St Duthac's, Tain was under the patronage of the Earls of Ross. In Caithness, what we now refer to as the St Magnus Chapel at Spittal is first recorded as the 'poors hospital' in 1290, founded by the Earls of Caithness. Magnus himself would have been aware of the practice of Orkney people going on pilgrimage to Tain and may well have supported the chapel, hence it's name. In return for supporting the cathedral, the political leaders would be guaranteed prayers for themselves and their family. In the case of influential bishops, some of whom spent more time at the royal court than in their cathedrals, they would also gain political influence.

Two inter-connected Saints

The Northern Pilgrims' Way is more than a modern way of linking two important pilgrimage sites in one journey. It is unusual in that the patron saint of our starting point in Tain, Saint Duthac, also had strong links with our end point on Orkney and the patron saint of our end point at St Magnus Cathedral, Orkney may well have had a devotion to Duthac[17]. So, whether you decide to travel from north to south or south to north, you are walking in the footsteps of previous pilgrims. There is ample historical evidence that pilgrims walked from Orkney to St Duthac's, Tain and from the south to St Magnus' Cathedral, Orkney. They will have taken slightly different routes, depending on the winds and tides, the season of the year or any relatives that they wanted to visit on the way but we are confident that the majority of these pilgrims would have walked the routes that we have mapped out.

Modern pilgrimages to ancient sites have their own restrictions and are adaptations of the journeys made by earlier travellers. So we have used a combination of five methods to work out a modern pilgrimage way that is true to the paths trod by those original pilgrims but avoids modern hazards. These methods were:

1. Folk memory and old tales
2. Assume that more modern routes follow ancient ones

---

[17] See the information on Spittal, below.

3. Use place names, chapel sites etc. as clues
4. Look at a map and plot a route that links the start and end points, while avoiding natural obstacles such as high mountains, deep rivers or dangerous bogs.
5. In the interests of safety, we made the policy decision to stick to existing paths

In the interests of simplicity, we describe the route from south to north but the original pilgrims would have been just as likely to go from north to south and the modern pilgrim is welcome to do so also.

There is a very plausible argument that the ancient pilgrimage routes, which would have followed everyday routes used for work and leisure, can be reconstructed by linking the ancient chapel sites. Specifically, chapels at the banks of rivers seem to consistently occur at fording points.[18] The rivers were significant influences on travel routes. They were reliable navigational aids but they were also natural barriers and had limited crossing points. No main bridges existed north of Inverness until the beginning of the 19th century.[19] So fords, consisting of stepping

---

18 See work done by George Watson 'Roads and Tracks through Local History Part 3' in the Caithness Field Club archives, available on-line.
19 From 1804 to 1821, Thomas Telford supervised the construction of roads and bridges throughout the Highlands and it was another 30 years after that before the north west coast was connected to this network.

stones, turf mounds or natural shallows that could be waded through, were used. These occurred most frequently near the sources of the rivers or at their mouths. Where rivers were too deep to allow for fords or simply wading, it is possible that coracles could have been used.

Rivers and burns were also popular sites for buildings designed to house groups of people larger than the average family. There were two reasons for this – they provided a convenient source of water for cooking and washing and they made it easier to dispose of waste in a hygienic manner. While there do not seem to be any remaining examples of toilets built over burns on our route, this was a common arrangement in other parts of the country and there is no reason why it could not also have been used here.
The larger rivers may well have been used as both navigational aids and for coracles to reduce mileages on foot or simply at crossing points. Sea travel would have been common but the traditional pilgrim would have been expected to walk. The historical evidence suggests that most pilgrims would have followed the coast, or at least stayed fairly close to it, as far as Helmsdale, then branched inland for a few miles to Kilphedar, crossed over to Braemore and continued via Dalnawillan, Dalnaha, and Achscoraclate to Spittal. From there they could reach the coast via Halkirk or Watten, both important centres. Dunbeath was also an important centre, so pilgrims could have continued along the coast and branched inland to Braemore from there. In the end, the group decided to

use the fairly new long-distance coastal walk from Inverness to John O'Groats, which passes through Tain, and create three options or 'braids' to allow for different interests and walking abilities. All braids follow the John O'Groats Trail from St Duthac's, Tain to Helmsdale. Then Braid One branches inland but continues past Kilphedar, as the crossing from there to Braemore is unmarked and very boggy. So the modern pilgrim stays on the road (or the fishermen's riverside track in places), passes through Kildonan, a very important centre in the 7th century, and on to the edge of the Flow Country, turning eastward at Forsinain because that is where a modern forestry track takes them to Loch More.

On the principle that more modern tracks follow older ones, it is possible that this section may have been used by pilgrims coming from/going to points to the west of Thurso. Some maps show the *Ca na Catanach* track. The name means 'Way of the Southern men' and is mentioned in histories of the feuds and cattle raids between the MacKays to the south and the Gunns to the north of the Caithness/Sutherland border. It was later used in the perfectly legitimate 19th century cattle droving trade. These tracks still exist in some areas but have been covered by forestry in others.

Having decided that the Kilphedar to Braemore route was now too dangerous, our next-best option was just to continue to Dunbeath and reach Braemore from there. This became Braid Two and is probably the most authentic of our braids. Before the modern A9, this route was the standard road to Thurso and is described on some maps as 'the old road to Thurso'. What now are remote scattered houses would once have been busy communities, taking advantage of the comparatively level and fertile ground. Braid Two joins Braid One on the north coast of Loch More. This is another modern adaptation, as the original route would have turned east at Dalnaha (the name means 'the meadow of the ford'[20]) and followed the southerly shore of the loch, passing by or even staying overnight at St Bridget's Chapel and Holy Well at Achscoraclate before crossing the river again at Dirlot. We regretfully stayed with the northerly option as the south side of the loch is dangerously boggy.

Originally, we were going to have what is now Braid Two as the only option as far as Spittal and then have three branches going to the three ferries – Scrabster via Halkirk and Skinnet; Gills Bay via Watten and Canisbay; John O'Groats (summer only) via Watten and Canisbay. Following various discussions, we have ended up with three options between Tain and Spittal but only one option from there to the coast! How did this happen? Well, the braid just described has the disadvantage of passing through a private sporting estate. In order to safely go

---

[20] This name is interesting in that it is a rare example of a word that has been adopted from Pictish to Gaelic, (Information from a talk by Guto Rhys for the Pictish Arts Society). The initial 'Dal' is rare in places with a Norse influence, so is not derived from the Norse 'dair'. See Watson p.414.

about the estate business, there are locked gates at both the Braemore and Loch More ends. These allow walkers and cyclists but not motor vehicles and are 16 miles apart. So a pilgrim using this braid needs to be confident of being able to walk this distance (and more if they do not have a drop-off and pick-up arrangement) without any back-up. Also, even walkers are banned at certain times, so an alternative seemed to be necessary. Braid One was added mainly because it has a reasonable historical authenticity and can be combined with using the train to break it up into reasonable sections. Then Braid Three, which simply follows the John O'Groats Trail, was included partly just because it is there and we use it for the first section, partly for those who might not feel up to going too far from their overnight stops and public transport. While it was probably not used very much by long-distance pilgrims (remember those bridgeless rivers!), it has many ancient chapel sites, holy wells and even older brochs to provide links with the past.

It was pointed out that using three options from Spittal to the coast may be historically accurate but it would add considerably to the complexity of the route, not to mention the problems of signage! So we agreed on Gills Bay as it is close to the area around Ham and John O'Groats, which local tradition identifies as the most popular crossing point in medieval times. It is also shorter and cheaper than the Scrabster crossing. The Gills Bay ferry takes you to St Margaret's Hope, South Ronaldsay, Orkney. Then there is another adaptation for safety reasons – please just take the bus for the 15 miles into Kirkwall as the causeways linking the islands do not have pedestrian walkways and are dangerous for walkers. The original pilgrims would have continued by boat into Scapa Bay and landed almost at the steps of the cathedral, which was much closer to the shore then than it is now. Perhaps some day an enterprising firm will run a boat charter business for use by pilgrims. Also in the future, it may be possible to walk from the end of the last causeway at St Mary's by a coastal path into Kirkwall but at the time of writing, this involves climbing over barbed-wire fences and a section along the bottom of a cliff that can only be accessed at low tide. We cannot recommend this!

Purists who wish to walk the Orkney section of the route have the option of going from Spittal to Scrabster via Halkirk and Thurso. This has several advantages – they could visit the sites at Skinnet and Thurso and, once on Orkney, they could join the St Magnus Way, a walking route into Kirkwall. The Scrabster ferry lands at Stromness on the Orkney mainland. To join the St Magnus Way, check the notes in the section 'Gills Bay and Beyond' under the heading 'Following Braid One'.

So that is how we ended up with three braids between Tain and Spittal but only one from there to Kirkwall. To help you to decide which braid to take, I will now describe the various towns, villages and historic sites on the way. The information given for each site is not meant to be exhaustive but to give you a feel for the place. I have concentrated on the pre-

Reformation (up to mid-15th Century) history and, even then, ignored much of the secular events.

Once in Caithness, i.e. from around Forsinain on Braid One and the Ord of Caithness on Braids Two and Three, the Northern Saints Trails group hope that you will stay for a few days and explore the area by following their six trails. Details of these can be found in Part Three of this work. There is much to see!

St Duthac's Collegiate Church, Tain

PART TWO: a Braided Route
Now those who were scattered went about preaching the good news. (Acts 8:4)

Some hints on travelling in the Highlands
First, let me flag up a point drawn to my attention recently – the Scottish countryside regulations, commonly known as the 'right to roam' say that dogs must be kept under strict control. Please interpret this as 'must be kept on a lead at all times'. Walkers on our route will be going through farm land, with the fairly obvious risks attached to mixing farm animals and domestic dogs. They will also be going through wide open spaces, home to ground-nesting birds and other wildlife.

The Northern Pilgrims' Way has been designed for walkers and details of the various stages are given on the website and in the guidebook, obtainable through the website. Some pilgrims may have motorised back-up. If this is provided by people who are not used to driving on singe-track roads, I ask that they ensure that the drivers involved are familiar with the following advice.

The Northern Saints Trails, while originally designed for car drivers, are very suitable for cyclists. Some stretches can even be walked. However I am assuming that the majority of travellers will be driving. Many of the roads mentioned are single-track and it is important to adapt your driving accordingly. The following is taken from the Highway Code:

Rule 155: **Single-track roads.**
These are only wide enough for one vehicle. They may have special passing places. If you see a vehicle coming towards you, or the driver behind wants to overtake, pull into a passing place on your left, or wait opposite a passing place on your right. Give way to road users coming uphill whenever you can. If necessary, reverse until you reach a passing place to let the other vehicle pass. Slow down when passing pedestrians, cyclists and horse riders.

In addition, here are a few tips:

- If you are unsure of your reversing abilities, take a few lessons before your journey
- passing places are usually marked by white diamond-shaped signs. If you have several cars on your tail or the car behind is crowding you, pull into a passing place and let them overtake. If the nearest passing place is on your right, stop opposite it and let the other car pass you by going into the passing place.
- Remember that you are on holiday, with time to spare, but the car behind you may not be so lucky. The local GP/district nurse/harassed mother/delivery driver on a tight schedule will appreciate your courtesy in pulling in and letting them pass.
- When cars are approaching each other, the rule is that the car nearest to a passing place stops there and lets the other car past. If one car has to reverse, it should be the one nearest to a passing place. If

the oncoming car flashes its lights, this is an unofficial signal to say that they want you to proceed.

- On hills, the upcoming traffic has priority (but also consider the distance from a passing place for each car).
- Do not expect a vehicle towing a caravan/trailer/farm implement to reverse even if they are the closest to a passing place
- Do not stop on the road, no matter how stunning the view or appealing the Highland cattle – continue to the next passing place, park the car and walk back, but only if there is still space in the passing place for another vehicle to pull in! Do not attempt to touch animals, wild or domestic.
- If you want to leave your car in a passing place for a few minutes, make sure that there is enough space left for another vehicle to pull in to allow passing/overtaking
- If you hear a siren, pull into a passing place as soon as possible as an emergency vehicle is trying to get through.
- Do not let the fuel tank get low – it may be quite a long drive to the next source of fuel. Few garages are open in the evenings and Sunday trading is still uncommon in many areas.
- Public toilets are also scarce – make the most of any that you see.

If you take a walk off the road, do not be tempted to swim, paddle or collect wild flowers from any of the small lochans – they have very soft, muddy bottoms and you could sink a surprising distance into them.[21] There have been cases of people disappearing altogether. Also, it is illegal to pick wild flowers. Even the surrounding bogs can be dangerous, being far less solid than they look! Walking off-road also incurs the risk of picking up a tick (those small black blood-sucking insects that attach themselves to any exposed skin. While they are normally harmless, they can cause Lymes Disease and must be removed with care. A special tool for the purpose can be bought at most chemists and is a useful addition to the standard first aid kit.

Many of our sites are on farm land. In order not to tarnish the post-mortem reputations of our saints, please do not do anything to upset the farmer/crofter/landowner. All the standard Country Code rules apply[22]. In addition, please remember the following:

- while there is a Freedom to Roam law in Scotland that allows the public access to all land, other than private gardens, as long as they are not doing any damage, this must be applied with courtesy to-wards the farmer/crofter/landowner

21   For anyone interested in wild swimming, see the table of safe and unsafe inland waters in Part Three.

22   See www.outdooraccess-scotland.com for details.

- another law guarantees the public's right of access to graveyards, even private ones. We have tried to identify the least-intrusive access routes and to gain the co-operation of the farmer/crofter/landowner. Sometimes the site is in the middle of a field and access cannot be guaranteed without disturbing stock or damaging crops. You may wish to just view from afar or, if you really want to stand on the site, please consult the local farmer/crofter/landowner first.

And last but by no means least – the Highland midge. If you are travelling between mid-June and mid-September, remember to take insect repellent with you. You might want to consider buying a midge hood that provides a net over the face. Midges thrive in the cool, damp climate of the North and West of Scotland. (The West-coast midges have been scientifically proven to be the most vicious in the world!) While they do not carry diseases, they can force the most stoic person indoors and ruin any outdoor pursuit. Some people are more sensitive to their bites than others but it is rare to be totally immune and even born-and-bred locals do not build up an immunity. Fortunately, they do not like hot, sunny weather or strong winds. While sunlight cannot be guaranteed, our routes do have more than their fair share of wind, so the midge is not a permanent problem.

The midge is not the only form of wildlife in the area, as the next few notes show.

Flora and Fauna

I do not know enough about this topic to go into any detail but can highlight a few things to look out for.

The first stages of out route follow the coast, where dolphins are sometimes seen and seals are regular sunbathers on the rocks. Seals are curious creatures and will sometimes swim along in parallel with you. If you sing to them, they may come closer! Once you reach the Pentland Firth, killer whales can occasionally be seen from the ferry.

As you travel north, you will pass by dramatic cliffs that are home to many seabirds – various gulls, guillemots, gannets, skuas to name a few. A few cliffs in Caithness provide nesting sites for puffins but these can only be seen during the breeding season in late spring/early summer.

On the inland sections, look out for buzzards circling overhead. In the spring, the evocative call of the curlew can still be heard. Nearer farmland, there will be a mixture of rooks and crows. The area round Forsinard – the Flow Country – is rich in many forms of life – wading birds, insects, peat-loving plants. Its main claim to fame is the peat itself. This forms a blanket bog and Forsinard has one of the largest blanket bogs in the world, storing more carbon than if the whole of the British Isles were covered in trees. For this reason, there is a bid in progress to have the area declared a World Heritage Site. Much of the area is owned by the RSPB and they have a visitor centre at Forsinard. The name comes from the Norse 'floi' meaning 'wet' and pronounced to rhyme with 'cow'.

The only larger wild animal that you are likely to see is the red deer. In Wick and Thurso, you may be lucky enough to see otters at the river mouths.

Plant life is much as you would expect in peaty soil – heather, bracken, rushes and the almost constantly flowering yellow gorse. Look closer and you might see various orchids. Once in Caithness and at the right time of year, a few sites are home to the rare Scottish primrose. For a picture and lots more go to the caithness.org website, listed below. A very few sites are home to the even rarer great yellow bumblebee.

For those of you who would like to know more, here are some sources.

On the Flow Country:
www.theflowcountry.org.uk, and
https://www.rspb.org.uk.reserves-a-z-flows

On plant life:
https://www.caithness.org/nature/plantsincaithness/index.htm. and
https://www.plantlife.org.uk/uk/nature-reserves-important-plant-areas/nature-reserves/munsary-peatlands (At the time of writing, the Munsary site is not open to the public as the ecosystem is very fragile.)

Various relevant articles: Caithness Field Club articles, found at htpps://www.caithness.org
Ken Butler and Ken Crossan: Wild Flowers of the North Highlands of Scotland
I

If you are in the area, Castletown Heritage Centre has information on the local habitat and the flagstone industry that was so important to both Castletown and Spittal.

You could also contact the Highland Council rangers service (run by Highlife Highland) at https://www.highlifehighland.com/ for information on guided walks and other outdoor activities.

Following Braid One

In the following descriptions, various historical sites are marked on the Highland Environmental Records (abbreviated to HER) map managed by Highland Council. I have included the map references for many of them, which take the form 'ND' followed by two four-digit numbers. The map can be found at

https://her.highland.gov.uk/map

I have also added the site number for those places that overlap with the Northern Saints Trails.

Tain

Saints: Mary, Duthac

The modern Royal Burgh of Tain, the oldest royal borough in Scotland, lies on a loop road off the busy A9 on the south coast of the Dornoch Firth. One theory as to the origins of the name is that it comes from the Norse 'Thing', signifying a place for local dignitaries to meet to discuss the important issues of the day. Its location close to an important water-way means that it has been easily accessible since the age of the coracle, so Viking long-ships would have had no problem in reaching it. Another theory is that the town is named after the river, using the ancient British word for river, as in the Tay, Tyne etc. As the language of the Picts seems to have been very close to early British, this is plausible.

Tain's main claim to fame is that St Duthac was born and brought up here in the early 11th century. The town very much sees itself as a sanctuary and pilgrimage centre and is proud of its long history as such. Much of this history, including three carved stones, can be found at the Tain and District Museum. For details of the stones, go to https://highlandpictishtrail.co.uk/project/tain-museum/.

Tain has three chapel sites dedicated to Duthac. The first was built on what was thought to be his birth place. Its ruins can still be seen in the old graveyard near the golf course. When St Duthac's relics were returned from Ireland, a second chapel was built to house them, under the governance of the monks of Fearn Abbey. The chapel had the official status of a sanctuary. This was famously breached when Robert the Bruce (1274-1329) was fighting to claim the Scottish throne and his wife and daughters took sanctuary in St Duthac's chapel, only to be forcibly removed and imprisoned by supporters of John Balliol, the other main claimant to the throne. The building itself was burned down in 1427 during a feud between the Clan MacKay and the Mowats, when one side ingeniously side-stepped the rule of sanctuary by setting fire to it. Fortunately for St Duthac's relics, the work of building a larger church had begun in 1370 to cope with the numbers of pilgrims. The relics were transferred there and it became St Duthac's Collegiate Church. In 1492, this church's collegiate status was confirmed by Pope Innocent VIII. The papal bull can still be seen in the museum and the Collegiate Church still stands in pride of place in the centre of the town.

The most famous pilgrim was King James IV

(1473-1513) who visited Tain at least once a year, and sometimes more, for twenty years. While his motives may have been as much secular as religious (these journeys included visits to important local leaders along the way and maintained his popularity with everyone), they did wonders for Tain's reputation as an important pilgrimage centre.

At the Reformation, pilgrimages were banned and the relics of St Duthac disappeared. Despite this, the local people could not bring themselves to destroy the statue of him in the church and he is still regarded as the patron saint of Tain. The modern town continues to look after the collegiate church and the museum beside it that is well worth a visit. School children are taught about St Duthac and have a 'St Duthac's week' in the spring every year, to coincide with his feast day on 8th March. Tain has a proud record for education. Tain Royal Academy, founded in 1813 was the only academy north of Inverness until 1914 and took boarders from across the Highlands. It was established by a royal charter from George III, confirmed by the Princess Royal on her visit in 2013.

The only other religious site is a well dedicated to Mary. It lies on the borough boundary about ½ mile north of the town on the seashore. According to the Canmore website, it

> 'is marked by a boundary stone and two fallen stone blocks. About half a mile north of Tain, by the sea shore, and well under high water mark, is a spring dedicated to the Virgin. Its waters were a remedy for consumption, but they had to be drunk on the spot, and as early

in the morning as the state of the tide allowed.[23]

A more secular site that the visitor might find interesting is the Glenmorangie Distillery, conveniently situated near the pilgrimage route as it leaves the town in the direction of the Dornoch Bridge. They even produce a single malt called 'St Duthac'![24]

Dornoch
Saints: Finbar; Gilbert; James; Francis;
Site number 27 on the NST

Today, Dornoch is best known as a golfing centre. On a loop road from the busy A9 and close to the sea, it has an air of quiet prosperity. This sense of peace and quiet is not caused by the cathedral but was one of the reasons why the cathedral was built there in the first place.

During the 1130's and 40's King David I worked to reorganise the diocesan structure of Scotland. In 1150, he moved Bishop Andrew from Dunfermline to Caithness, Ross and Moray. The bishop was officially based in Elgin but had plans to build a new cathedral in Dornoch. He wanted a religious community in Dunfermline to establish a centre in Dornoch but that is as far as his plans went.

---

[23] http://canmore.rcahms.gov.uk/
[24] At the time of writing, this was only available at foreign airports.

In 1222 Bishop Adam of Caithness was burned alive in Braal Castle, Halkirk by some angry farmers in a dispute over taxes that he was trying to collect on behalf of the landowners. His successor, Gilbert of Moravia, felt uneasy, with the farmers on one side and the Norse on the other. As he had been gifted land further south, he moved to Dornoch, which already had a monastic settlement. He founded the cathedral there in 1224 and this remained his episcopal seat. However he continued to travel around his diocese and died back in Caithness (of natural causes!) in 1245. The cathedral had been built beside an existing chapel dedicated to the Caithness-born St Finbar, so Gilbert dedicated the cathedral to him but it was re-dedicated to Gilbert after his death.

Dornoch is also famous as the last site of a legal killing of a woman, Janet Horne, as a witch in June 1727. Janet's daughter had a deformity of her hands and feet, so neighbours decided that these were actually hooves and Janet used her daughter to ride around the countryside at night. There is now a memorial stone marking the site where she was burned to death.

The dedication to James refers to a side altar in the cathedral dedicated to him. The link with St Francis is less clear but there seems to have been a convent in the area dedicated to him, as there was in Wick.

For more information on the history of the area, visit the Historylinks Museum.

As you approach Golspie along Ferry Road, look out for stone markers for the Battle of Little

Ferry (1746). For details go to
www.facebook.com/BattleofLittleferry/ or
www.spanglefish.com/golspieheritagesociety/.

Golspie
Saints: Malie, Andrew   site number 26 on the
NST.

The name 'Golspie' is Norse for 'gully village',
suggesting that the early inhabitants lived further
inland than the existing houses. Golspie is best
known to local travellers as a convenient stopping
point, with a car park, public toilets and coffee shop
conveniently situated together just off the main road
in the centre of the town. For visitors, there are an
attractive beach, the Big Burn walk and Ben
Bhraggie for the walkers and Dunrobin Castle for
those less active. Within the castle grounds is a small
museum with a locally-sourced collection of about
twenty Pictish carved stones For details, go to
https://highlandpictishtrail.co.uk/project/dunrobin-
castle-museum/.

      Both Ben Bhraggie and the castle elicit mixed
feelings among those with a knowledge of local
history, associated as they are with the notorious
Highland Clearances. The summit of Ben Bhraggie
has a statue of the Duke of Sutherland which
dominates the skyline. Originally built to honour the
memory of the first Duke of Sutherland (d.1833), it
has become instead a reminder of the role played by
the duke and, even more so, his wife in clearing over
2,000 crofters from their Sutherland estates in the

early 19th century. Their family seat, which the countess visited annually from London, was Dunrobin Castle. Now open to the public, visitors can admire the stately rooms and beautiful gardens. For some, their beauty is spoilt by the thought of the human misery that was the price paid for this display of wealth and privilege.

A recent documentary quoted a church leader as saying that the crofters had been told by the local ministers that they were being punished for their sins and should accept this humbly. This is not quite the whole story. Church of Scotland ministers often owed their positions to the local landlord and some may have had divided loyalties. However many Free Church of Scotland ministers protested at the treatment of their flock and joined those that emigrated in order to give them spiritual support in their new lives.

To return to earlier years, Golspie was associated with the name Malie, of whom nothing is known. The old name of Golspie parish was Kilmaly, possibly from *cuil Mhaillidh* 'Maillie's retreat'. The Church of Scotland is dedicated to St Andrew. The graveyard had a large cross-slab with both Pictish symbols and Ogham characters on it. This is now in the Dunrobin Castle Museum. Also in the Dunrobin Museum are various artifacts from the Cairn Liath broch which is just north of Golspie between the main road and the sea. This broch is easily accessible and still has interesting features to explore. For details of the professional surveys, go to the HER map, reference NC8703 0137.

For anyone interested in the history of the Sutherland clearances, try doing an internet search for Elizabeth Levison-Gower, Duchess of Sutherland. For more general local history, visit the Golspie Heritage Museum, already mentioned.

Brora

Saints: Faolin, Iain, Columba, Peter, Mirren, The Brethren.   Site number 25 on the NST.

The modern town of Brora also has links with the Sutherland clearances as it is part of the same estate. It is unusual for a Highland village in that it has an industrial history, starting with salt pans. Then coal mining began in the late 16th century. This continued on a small scale until the late 18th century and was re-vived in 1811 to provide employment for the dis-placed crofters. Despite the thin seams and a coal type that was prone to bursting into flames, the mine, the most northerly one in Britain, continued until 1974. Another industry, directly linked to the clearances and the introduction of large-scale sheep farming, was the Brora Woollen Mill, later known as Hunters of Brora, (1837 to 2003). Crofters from across the Highlands sent their raw fleeces there, to be returned as knitting wool.

The industry most directly connected to our story is the Clyneleash Distillery. First built in 1819, it has passed through various owners and moved from one building to another but is still thriving and is worth a visit. The connection with the pilgrimage route is more to do with its location than its product –

the area is associated with the names of various early saints – Faolan, Iain, Columba, Peter. Watson mentions seven churches in Strathbrora – *Kilnabraar* (the brethren's church where the brethren could be Peter and Andrew or James and John); *Cill Pheadair Mhor (The big church of Peter); Cill Pheadair Bheag (the small church of Peter); Cill Chaluim Chille* (St Columba's, but see below and 'Colum' in the Alphabetical List of Saints. If this is a dedication to Columba, it is the only one on the east coast); *Cill Eathain* (St. John's); *Cill Mhearain* (St. Mirren's) and *Cill Ach-Breanaidh*.[25]

Little is known about Faolin but the parish church at Clyne had a dedication to him. Iain is better-known as he is listed as a follower of Donan and one of the Eigg martyrs (see the entry under 'Kildonan' for more details.) The Columba link could be due to one of his followers coming to the area but could also be a mis-understanding. Columba himself did not travel so far north but there were several more local, but not well-known, saints with names that later historians could assume to be corruptions of 'Columba' – Colm, Colum and Coomb all have Caithness connections and may, or may not, be one person. The dedication to Peter is simpler to explain. Curitan (7th century) took the name Boniface and was based on the Black Isle but travelled around the north. He had a devotion to Peter as there was a family tradition that they were descended from Radia, Peter's sister. So he replaced dedications to earlier saints with ones to Peter.

---

[25] See Watson p.275

Three miles north of Brora is Kintradwell in the parish of Loth, an area rich in history. A broch[26] near the shore is evidence that this area was inhabited long before the period in which we are interested. There was a strong local tradition that, slightly further inland and just south of the present Kintradwell House, was a chapel dedicated to one of the few female saints of the Celtic period. She is also one with the greatest number of alternative names – Triduana, Trinuan, Trolla, Trollen, Trollhena (and Trolhena of the Sagas), Tredwen, Tredwell, Trullen. Tradition says that she came from Achaia with St Regulus when he brought the bones of St Andrew to Scotland in the 4th century (or possibly the 7th century). Her main shrine is in Restalrig, Edinburgh, where the name 'Triduana' is used. There was no trace of the Kintradwell chapel – until 2000/2001when a new water main was being installed at Kintradwell House and the driver of the digger opening the trench realised that he was digging up human bones. Further investigation showed that this was the missing chapel and graveyard. Sixteen skeletons were removed and dated to the 10th Century. The site is marked on the HER map with reference no NC 9221 0741.

The name 'Kintradwell' is also debated. It may be a corruption of an earlier 'Cill Trollen' as the prefix 'Cill' suggests a chapel site. It may also be a modernisation of the name of the nearby farm – 'Kentrulla', (or Cuin Trolla/ Cill-Trolla / Clen Trolla

---

[26] If you are wondering what a broch is, go to www.thebrochproject.co.uk

– Trolla's headland). There seems little doubt that the area was a significant religious centre in Celtic times as five carved crosses have been found there. Some are in the Dunrobin Museum but some have got lost.

The pilgrim's next stop is Helmsdale. If travelling on the A9 rather than the JOGT, you will come to a layby at Lothbeg near where a minor road branches off to the left. In the layby is a memorial stone to the last wolf in Sutherland, killed in 1700.

For those staying on the JOGT, follow the coast to Portgower, where the route takes you on a loop inland towards Gartymore. Near-by is the site of a chapel dedicated to Saint Inan (ND 0124 1428). This was built by the wife of the then Earl of Sutherland, Lady Margaret Baillie, in the late 15th Century. As St Inan belonged to Ayrshire and had no known links with Sutherland, it seems likely that Lady Margaret, who came from Ayrshire, brought a devotion to the saint with her.

The loop continues into Helmsdale.

Helmsdale
Saints; John   site number 24 on the NST

The modern village of Helmsdale owes its prosperity to the fishing industry of the 19th century and the ongoing salmon fishing on the river that runs through the centre of the village. The correct name of the river and its strath is 'Ilidh' or 'Ullidh', meaning 'flood', but the river is more commonly known as the Helmsdale River and the strath as the Strath of Kildonan.

The river was first bridged by Thomas Telford in 1811 (not the current A9 bridge) and a planned village followed a few years later to accommodate those cleared from the strath to make way for sheep. However the area was inhabited long before this. The bay made a natural harbour for travellers, both Viking and earlier, and the wide strath took the traveller, possibly by coracle on the river, well inland and within reach of Loch More, Thurso River and on to the coast. Archaeological remains suggest that the area was well-populated, with the river and its surrounding fertile banks providing food for human and animal alike.

The main dedication in Helmsdale is to John the Baptist. The outline of the mediaeval Saint John's Hospice can still be seen in the graveyard of the current St John's Church. It was originally the site of Iain's cell, one of Donnan's disciples, but fell into disuse on the departure of Donan and his followers. The existence of a hospice/hostel indicates that Helmsdale was an important pilgrimage centre.

Sometime before 1357, the church was restored, re-dedicated to St John and erected as a Hospital and Ferry House for Travellers. The management of the establishment proved unsatisfactory and William de Moravia, the Fourth Earl of Sutherland, put the Hospital and ferry into the possession and care of the Monastery of Kinloss. (The Earls originally came from Moray.) The Hospital was called the "Hospital of Saint John the Baptist", and the monastery at Kinloss always supplied Saint John's with two monks, sometimes more, and their servants.

The Church and Hospital were endowed with lands and fishings, and the church later became a Chapel of Ease under the Church of Loth. Up to the Reformation the church was still supplied by Morayshire clergy, and was in use until about 1820, when the roof gave way.

Saint John's Well is across the river from the church site. It is the only well in Scotland dedicated to John the Baptist - a unique piece of the Northern Pilgrims' Way history, as other Saint John's are named after the Evangelist. The reason is unknown - maybe it was the position of the church, the river and the well - but perhaps the explanation for the dedication is buried in ancient Church records in Moray, still waiting to be discovered. It is also possible that the dedication was chosen in memory of Iain as 'Iain' is the Gaelic form of 'John'.

There is a chapel site dedicated to Rect/Rectaire on the hill to the north-west of the village. Rect was a follower of Donnan of Kildonan and was with him when he and his group were martyred on the Island of Eigg.

Helmsdale played a part in one of Scotland's many historical tragedies. On 3rd October 1290 a group of English envoys spent a night here on their way to meet the Maid of Norway. The daughter of the king of Norway, this eight-year-old girl was the only surviving heir to her maternal grandfather, King Alexander III of Scotland and was also a granddaughter of King Henry III of England. After the death of Alexander in 1286 a treaty was agreed between Scotland and England that Margaret would marry Edward's son and heir, thus uniting the two kingdoms. Scotland would retain political and legal independence. When word reached Edward that Margaret was on her way to Scotland, he sent envoys to meet her. However a storm blew her ship off-course and it landed at St Margaret's Hope, Orkney instead of the Scottish mainland. Margaret died there, possibly as the result of severe sea-sickness, leaving Robert Bruce and John Balliol, already mentioned in connection with sanctuary in St Duthac's, Tain, to begin their struggles to claim the empty Scottish throne.

The local museum, Timespan, gives an excellent introduction to the history of the area. Find out more about it at https://highlandpictishtrail.co.uk/project/timespan/.

Here is a summary of the various sites in the area, with their HER reference.

St Peter's Chapel   NC 9897 2046

Kilphedir   NC 9880 1860

St Ernan's Chapel and Cemetery   NC 9200 1800

St Donan's Chair   NC 9495 1872

St John the Baptist Well, Chapel, Hospital, ND 0256 1565

Holy Well, Glen Loth   NC 9354 1305)   St Iain's (?John) Chapel, Gartmore   ND 0125 1427

St Ninian's Chapel and Cemetery, Navidale   ND 0419 1614, ND 0419 1615,

St Rect's Chapel, Navidale   ND 0300 1600 (Rect=Rectair/Reet)

At Helmsdale, Braid One of the NPW turns west and follows Strath Ullidh, or the Strath of Kildonan as it is usually known, inland to Kildonan and Forsinard. The following description is of a point between Helmsdale and Kildonan but I have been unable to identify it on the HER map.

> On the way, you will pass a section of the river going through an area called Achahemisgach on the East side and Learabail on the opposite bank. The East side of the river has a rock with a cross carved on it. The adjacent wood is called Coille Chil Mer or 'the wood of the cell of Mary'.[27]

About five miles along the road is Kilphedar. The name means 'the cell of Peter'. The original hermit would probably have come from the monastic settlement further up the strath and the name may well be one of those cases of 'Peter' replacing an earlier Celtic name. The original cell and chapel were further up the burn, the Allt Cille Pheadair, from the present road. This seems to have been a recognised way for travellers from Helmsdale and the surrounding area to cross over to Braemore, where there was another monastic site, and continue north through Caithness. While the low-lying ground is now very boggy and is too dangerous to recommend, it has evidence of hut circles, sheilings etc which mean that it was not always so. One example of its use, dated 1588, is when

---

[27] Donald Sage at 22% on the Kindle edition. 'Mary' may be a corruption of 'Maire', one of Donnan's followers.

the Earl of Sutherland and a large following, crossed over between Morven and Scaraben, following the Allt Cille Pheadair burn and camped overnight at Corriechoich, near Braemore, intent on laying Caithness to waste[28]. A more peaceful use of this route, dating from the 13th century, was to carry the coffins of members of the Clan Gunn to their traditional graveyard at St Magnus Chapel, Spittal.

The modern traveller must continue past Kilphedar on the road or riverside path towards Kildonan. As this is prime salmon-fishing territory, please do not disturb any fishermen on the path – they have paid dearly for their use of this stetch of the river and it would give pilgrimage and pilgrims a bad name if you disturbed them. Remember that the first apostles were fishermen and Jesus himself ate fish!

Kildonan
Saint: Donnan

[29]Donnan was an Irish Pict who came to Scotland to join the mission at Whithorn on the Solway Firth. He set out from there with 52 disciples c. 580 A.D. and travelled north. From his monastery at Kildonan, he

---

[28] See Calder's 'History of Caithness' for more details p. 132 and from p.93 for a history of the Clan Gunn

[29] The following three paragraphs are courtesy of Audrey Munro for her summary from 'The Pictish Nation its People and its Church' and 'Saint Donnan the Great and His Muinntir' by Rev. Dr. Archibald Black Scott.

sent missionaries to found churches all over the north of Scotland, from Caithness to Inverness-shire and even across the Moray Firth to Banff-shire. His name was so closely associated with the area that one of the ancient records mistakenly located his martyrdom there. He lives on in numerous local names – the whole strath being known as the Strath of Kildonan, rather than Strath Ullidh. its original Gaelic name.

Donnan was driven from Kildonan by the early Viking invaders a year or two before his death. When he left, he recalled his missionaries, and they all travelled to Wester Ross and the Inner Hebrides, founding more churches there, before settling on Eigg, where they were martyred by brigands (possibly on the orders of the local landlady) on Easter Day, 617 A.D. His mission had lasted 38 years and he became known as Saint Donnan the Great, an indication of his importance in the Celtic Church.

The church at Kildonan continued down the centuries and remained the parish church until after the Clearances. The present building dates from the 19th century and is built on the site of Donnan's cell, so today's visitors look out on the same fields, the same hills and the same river that Donnan contemplated fourteen hundred years ago.[30]

This part of the river is not only famous for its fish but was also the site of one of Scotland's gold-rushes. In 1868 a local man, Robert Gilchrist, who had

---

[30] To visit the church, turn left at the sign for Kildonan farm. The church is open and has information panels upstairs.

had experience in the Australian goldfields, discovered gold in the Helmsdale and Suisgill rivers. For the next fifty years, gold was panned from the river beds but this ended in 1869 when the Duke of Sutherland refused to issue any more licences and told the miners to clear their camps. This was partly the result of pressure from his tenant farmers and from fishermen, both more secure sources of income than the gold-panners. Today, it is again possible to get a licence to pan for gold but this is more as a holiday diversion than a serious attempt to make one's fortune. Information on the gold rush and how to obtain a licence is on a notice board at a car park beside the bridge over the river.

From Kildonan, the pilgrim continues along the strath, through Kinbrace to Forsinard (both of which have train stations but are request stops, so please check with Scotrail). There are the ruins of a chapel and graveyard at Ach'na H-uai, near Kinbrace train station but they seem to be of post-Reformation construction.

Forsinard, Loch More, Dirlot
Saints: Bridget, Colm Dirlot is site no 42 on the NST.

There are no known saints associated with Forsinard although priests from Kildonan would have passed through here on their way to and from the communities to the west of Thurso.

The area around Forsinard is owned and managed by the RSPB as it is home to several rare bird species due to the undisturbed peatbogs and small lochans. This is the Flow Country – the largest area of peatbog in the world. There is more carbon captured here than there would be if all of Britain was covered in forests. The RSPB run a visitor's centre at the station in the summer.

From Forsinard, the route continues for another four miles (6.5km) along the strath before turning east at Forsinain. From here to Loch More it follows forestry tracks, passing Altnabreac station on the way. There is an imposing building near the station. This was built as a shooting lodge in a previous age and is one of the reasons why the railway line meanders through the country instead of taking a direct line between Inverness and the north coast. When the railway company was seeking permission to build its track, the local landowners granted this on condition that the line went past their shooting lodges to make life easier for themselves and their guests.

At Loch More, the route joins a single-track tarred road that runs in an almost straight line to meet the A9 at Mybster. A couple of miles along this road, an even narrower road leads off to the right. About half a mile along, it ends at a farm steading. The gate to the right leads into a field and at the end of the field is Dirlot graveyard overlooking the River Thurso. As there may be sheep or cattle in the field, access to the graveyard is not guaranteed. It may be possible to use the left-hand field, go ahead to the river and back-track to the graveyard but this has not been tested and would again depend on whether or not there were livestock in the field.

The graveyard is built on the site of an early chapel dedicated to St Colm/Coomb/Colum. Some sources give Columba as the dedication but this is another example of later writers not being familiar with these early Celtic saints. Inside the graveyard there is an impressive figure marking one of the graves. This was carved by John Nicolson, a well-known Caithness farmer, painter and sculptor who accepted commissions for monuments and gravestones. He also excavated several local brochs in the late 19th and early 20th centuries.

On the opposite bank of the river are the remains of Dirlot Castle. There used to be a ford linking the two sites. The castle was built by Sir Reginald de Cheyne (d.1350), one of the signatories to the Declaration of Arbroath in 1320. He is buried at Olgrinbeg (site no 41 on the NST map).

The Dirlot ford is said to have treasure buried under it but please do not risk drowning by looking for it! A more negative story involves Reginald de Cheyne, who insisted that his baby daughters be drowned there because they were not sons. His wife instead sent them to the convent at Murkle (see under Catherine/Katherine in the Alphabetical List of Saints). When they had grown up, they attended a ball at the castle and their father was so taken by their beauty that his wife told him who they were and he acknowledged them as his daughters.

Between Dirlot and Loch More are a group of standing stones and another graveyard. See Braid Two for more information on them.

Braids One and Two now move on to Mybster crossroads, passing through Westerdale. At Westerdale, an old stone bridge crosses the River Thurso. Travellers heading to Halkirk and Thurso would have followed the river from here. Those going to the pilgrimage hostel, would have forded the river and continued up the hill to St Magnus Chapel, Spittal. The modern traveller continues on this minor road until it meets the A9. At the Mybster crossroads, Braids One and Two turn left along the A9 to Spittal. This means a short walk on the A9, so care is needed.

Spittal   saint: Magnus   site no 44 on the NST.

As you come into the village, the hall is on the left. At the time of writing there were plans to erect five information panels in the car park. These cover the various stages of life in the area over the last 2,000 years. First, there is a map and information on the brochs of Caithness, in use from about 500BC to the turn of the century. Then the Northern Saints Trails panel gives some idea of the early Christian period up to the 9th Century. The third panel shows that, from the 11th to 16th Centuries, the Northern Pilgrims' Way was in use. Caithness has always been good agricultural land and the fourth panel represent this with information on cattle droving, which took place during the 18th century. The last panel both brings us up-to-date and returns us to the earliest times. It is about the flagstone industry which has for many years turned the millions-of-years-old stone into fencing, walls, pavement slabs, fireplace surrounds and more. It is also a good source of fossils. The best source of these was at the Achanarras quarry, just inland from Spittal. This is signposted from the Westerdale – Mybster section of the road. (Achanarras also has a chapel site and a broch.)

By the time of the Celtic saints, Spittal was a well-known destination. Spittal Hill is the highest point in the area and was used to check the weather before deciding on what crossing to use between the coast and Orkney. The name of the village comes from the hospital/hostel (think 'hospitality') linked to the St Magnus Chapel on the outskirts of the village. As the name suggests, this was an important overnight resting point for pilgrims travelling between Tain and Kirkwall. One local tradition is that it got its name from pilgrims travelling to St Magnus Cathedral, another tradition is that St Magnus himself was a devotee of St Duthac and had the hostel and chapel built for fellow-travellers to Tain. The first written record of the chapel is in a royal charter from King James III to William Sinclair, Earl of Caithness in 1476 giving the earl patronage of the chapel plus various state offices. A second charter in 1566 confirmed that the lands around the chapel (Spittal, Achalone and Mybster) were attached to it. These lands would have been rented out and the revenue used to support the chapel and hostel.

There are still fairly substantial remains of the chapel and graveyard, which was in use until modern times as the traditional burial ground for the Clan Gunn. At the time of the clearances, many Gunns from

Strathnaver moved to Broubster and continued to use Spittal as their graveyard, the coffin route passing the 'House of Blessing' at Shurrery, Gavin's Kirk at Dorrery, St Peter's Chapel at Olgrinbeg and St Trostan's Chapel at the ford at Westerdale before arriving at St Magnus Chapel, Spittal.

While the chapel and graveyard are easily identified, there is dispute over the siting of the hostel, which some sources say pre-dated the chapel. Of the two surveys of the site, both identified the remains of a building close to the chapel. One concluded that this was the hostel site but the second one disputed this. If the hostel was not beside the chapel, the next most likely site is further up the hill where there are substantial ruins of what is now called the Spittal Byres or Spittal Dairy. This building was certainly used as a dairy, with living accommodation for the dairymaid, and could well have been used as an overnight shelter during the cattle droving days, when near-by Georgemas was a collecting point. However there are inconsistencies in the building that suggest an earlier usage. Only a full-scale archaeological study of both sites would give us a clearer picture. The remains of the chapel and the graveyard are only accessible via the steading of a working farm, so it is not possible for the pilgrim to visit the site. The Byres/Dairy are just off the A9 but are still on the farm land and do not have much to offer the visitor without an expert guide.

Spittal Hill used to be the site of an annual agricultural fair. There are records of one such fair in 1845, called the Jamesmas Fair and another in 1872, called the Georgemas Fair. The surrounding area is still called Georgemas. The change in name of the fair could be because of a change in the date of the fair, as they would normally be held around the name-saint's feast day. However, St George's feast day is 23rd April, which does not seem a likely date for an agricultural fair – too late for hiring seasonal workers, too early for selling produce.[31] Also, St George makes us think of England and dragons, not the north of Scotland, so why his name? One possible link is the crusades, which took place between the end of the 11th Century and the end of the 13th Century. St George was a popular saint among the crusaders. He lived in the 4th Century, spending some of his life in Palestine. He was a Christian in the Roman army and was beheaded for protesting at the persecution of Christians. His ghost is said to have helped the crusaders in their struggle to free the Holy Land. There are several links between the Crusades and the Earls of Caithness and Orkney (the St Clair's or Sinclairs). Here is a timeline showing links between the Sinclairs, the crusades, Orkney and Caithness, Denmark and Rosslyn chapel (famous for its 'Apprentice Pillar' and links with the Freemasons – the Sinclairs of Rosslyn were the hereditary heads of freemasonry in Scotland until 1736)[32].

---

[31] Just in case you are wondering , James' feast day is 25th July (assuming that we are talking about James the apostle)

[32] Despite many stories to the contrary, modern scholarship says that there are no links between Rosslyn Chapel and the Templars, who's last Grand Master was executed in 1314, over 100 years before the chapel was built. Similarly, there were no

1025-30 the original church at Roskilde was built (see below)

1058 to 1093 Malcolm Canmore, king of Scotland, and his successors grant large tracts of land to the Norman family of St Clair, including the baronies of Rosslyn

1096 Henry St Clair joins the first crusade

1309 Henry Sinclair (d.1330) in 1309 testifies against two Templars on trial in Edinburgh for heresy at the time of the disbanding of the order. The Templars, founded to protect pilgrims to the Holy Land, were neighbouring landowners of the Sinclairs near Rosslyn Chapel

1345 Henry Sinclair (d.1400) becomes Lord of Rosslyn

1379 Henry Sinclair, now Baron of Rosslyn, becomes the Earl of Orkney

1446 William Sinclair (1410-1484), 3rd Earl of Orkney and Caithness begins building Rosslyn Chapel to his own design

1455 William Sinclair becomes Earl of Caithness

1506 Sir David Sinclair of Sumburgh, Orkney left a gold chain (gifted to him from the king of Denmark) to St George's altar, Roskilde, Denmark in 1506. Roskilde was the Danish centre of devotion to St Magnus and celebrated his feast day on August 19th. It also had dedications to St George - St George's Hill on the outskirts of the town was named after a chapel and graveyard dedicated to St George. The graveyard had been

---

links between the Templars and Freemasonry, which was founded in Britain in 1550/60.

created for the victims of the plague in 1253. David was the 3rd son of William, Earl of Orkney and Caithness and grandson of Alexander Sutherland of Dunbeath, who had links with Rosslyn (1456).

1582 George Sinclair 4th Earl of Caithness was buried at Rosslyn Chapel.

So, with all these links between St George and the Sinclairs, it seems plausible that the original fair was called the Georgemas Fair and the surrounding area was named after the Fair.

We have wandered off the Northern Pilgrims Way route but not by very much. According to local tradition, there was a walking route, used even as late as the 1940's, that went through the village, past the site of the Spittal Byres and then turned right to skirt the northerly and easterly flanks of Spittal Hill and on to Watten. Partly for safety reasons and partly because this path includes farmers gates and fields, the modern route takes the pilgrim back to the crossroads at Mybster and along a minor road to Watten. This road passes an area called 'Markethill' which was probably where the Magnusmas fair was held. It also skirts the area of Dunn, so named after the Chapel of Dunn, but more on that when we reach our next stop, Watten itself.

While the official route goes from Spittal to Watten, an alternative with strong historical links is to reach the coast via Halkirk, Thurso and Scrabster. A ferry runs from Scrabster to Stromness, Orkney, from where the walker can join the St Magnus Way into Kirkwall.

Halkirk – Scotland's first planned village
Saints: Tarlogan; Fergus; Katherine;
site no 37 on the NST.

Halkirk was an important centre in the early church, with the bishop's palace at Braal, the chapel and carved stone at Skinnet just down the river and various saint's sites near-by. The name comes from the Norse 'Ha Kirkia', used in describing Bishop Adam's death in the Orkneyinga Saga, and is often translated as High Kirk but, as the churches at both Thurso and Skinnet were more important, this is disputed. Another possible translation uses 'low-lying' for 'Ha', giving us the information that the bishop's palace had been built on low-lying ground near an existing kirk. Braal Castle is certainly low-lying, being on the bank of the River Thurso.

For information on each saint, go to Part Four.

Thurso
Saint: Peter   site no 8 on the NST

There are two theories as to the origins of the name 'Thurso'. One is that it is a corruption of 'Thor's River', a reference to the Norse god. Another is that it comes from the Norse for 'bull's river'. Both theories acknowledge the Viking history of the area, going back to the 10th century. The main harbour at the other end of the bay from the town at Scrabster has always been busy, whether it be for Viking long-ships, the herring fishing fleet or modern ferries to Orkney. The bay itself has recently become home to a new activity – wind surfing. This bay and other local ones have some of the best surfing conditions in the world and have hosted the World Championships. What would the Vikings have made of that?

For the pilgrim, the main site of interest is Old St Peter's Kirk near the river mouth. For details of it, go to the entry on Peter in the Alphabetical List of Saints.

The modern Thurso owes its general atmosphere and prosperity to the Dounreay nuclear base further along the coast. This brought many young families to the area, well-paid jobs and apprenticeships for both local and incoming youngsters. The nuclear site is now being decommissioned but its history is traced in exhibitions at the North Coast Visitors Centre, Thurso, where there are also artefacts from Old St Peter's Kirk displayed beside the Skinnet and Ulbster stones.

Halkirk and Thurso are linked in the stories of Bishop John and Bishop Adam. I have taken the following account from the April 1982 edition of the Caithness Field Club's journal, to be found at https://www.Caithness.org

Two Tales of The Bishops of Caithness
Henrietta Munro
In the 12th century Earl Harold assumed control of Caithness. This was not to the liking of William the Lion so he arranged for Reginald Lord of

the Isles to recover the county for the king. This Reginald did this during Harold's absence in Orkney and then left the county under the charge of the bishop and three governors - at this time Harold was still in Orkney gathering up an army to recapture Caithness. Also at this time William the Lion had Harold's son tortured in Roxburgh Castle - Harold was sure the Bishop of Caithness had a great deal to do with this episode. So in 1201 Earl Harold landed at Scrabster with a very large army and the Bishop seeing the numbers, decided that appeasement was the only policy. When Harold was leaving Scrabster the Bishop left his palace and tried to make peace. Naturally Harold scornfully rejected the Bishop's plea and arrogantly asked where the money was - the money the Bishop was supposed to collect for the Earl which was one penny per inhabited house in Caithness. Regretfully the Bishop had to agree that he had failed to collect this tax. This of course did not improve Harold's temper and he instructed one of his servants - Lomberd by name - to cut out the Bishop's tongue and to thrust a knife into both his eyes.

After the dreadful deed was done, they left the Bishop beside the roadside, marched into Thurso and ravaged the town and then overran the countryside. Later Harold sued for pardon from the king and seems to have got off lightly but Lomberd was not so lucky. The Bishop of Orkney received a letter from the Pope as follows:

Lomberd shall hasten home and barefoot and naked except for breeches and a short woollen vest without sleeves, shall he have his tongue tied by a string and drawn out so as project beyond his lips and the ends of the string shall be bound round his neck and he shall have rods in his hands - in sight of all men he shall walk for fifteen days successively through his own native district, the district of the mutilated bishop and through the neighbouring county. He shall go to the door of the church - without entering - and there prostrate on the earth undergo discipline with the rods he is to carry. He is to spend each day in silence and fasting unto evening when he shall support nature with bread and water only. Then after these fifteen days have passed he shall prepare within a month to set out for Jerusalem and there labour in the service of the cross for three years. He shall further for a period of two years fast every Friday on bread and water unless under the indulgence of some discreet bishop or unless he be sick. He shall never more bear arms against Christians. Receive him in this manner and see that he observes the penance.

Unfortunately, there is no record of the outcome of this letter and we do not know whether the sentence was carried out or not.

THE MURDER OF BISHOP ADAM IN HALKIRK IN 1222

At this time the Norse earldom of Caithness and Orkney existed side by side and both made heavy claims on the predominantly Norse tenants of Halkirk. Although the Norse Earl John held Caithness from the King of Scots and not the King of Norway - to whom Orkney still belonged - it is likely that the bondi or farmers in Halkirk being of predominantly Norse descent, looked to Earl John as their rightful laird.

Anyway they came to him one day in his castle at Braal - the successor to which stands today on the north bank of the Thurso River just opposite the Abbey Kirk on the south side - and complained that Bishop Adam had increased his tiend imposts. Instead of twenty cows for a span of butter - this was a stone on Scots measure - he now wanted ten for every span. Earl John protested that it was none of his business but the farmers became very angry and to get rid of them the Earl is reported to have said, "Devil take the Bishop and his butter - you may roast him in it for all I care". And that is just what they did, The Bishop was drinking ale with the Sheriff in the upper room of the Episcopal Manse when the farmers entered and dragged him forcibly down to the kitchen, heaped more wood on the fire (some say butter as well) and burned the Bishop to death.

Alexander the First of Scotland at once marched to Caithness with an army and took vengeance on the murderers by mutilating a number of them and seizing their lands while for good measure the Pope excommunicated them in 1223.

There is also a story that some of the murderers were hanged at Gallowhill near Scrabster - this is supposed to be why the hill has this name.

Earl John who was the last of the Norse earls was himself murdered in Thurso in 1231.

So ends Henrietta Munro's telling of the stories of Bishops John and Adam. Let us move on!

Watten

Saints: Mary, Katherine, Fumac, Tarlogan, Bridget,
Magnus   site no 48 on the NST.

The modern village is best known for the fishing on
Loch Watten but it has several other claims to fame.

During World War II there was a military base
there. Towards the end of the war this was turned into
a prisoner-of-war camp. Due to its isolated setting, it
was used for several important prisoners who needed
a secure base. However many 'ordinary' prisoners
were housed there also and were used as free labour
on the near-by farms to replace the local men away at
war. There was generally a perfectly friendly
relationship between the prisoners and the locals.

Another claim to fame is that it was the
birthplace of the inventor, Alexander Bain (1811-
1877). Bain served his apprenticeship as a clockmaker
in Wick before moving to Edinburgh, London and
back to Edinburgh. While in London, he invented the
first electric clock, operated by a pendulum kept
moving by electromagnetism. Then he invented what
was in effect the first fax machine. He moved back to
Edinburgh and continued to invent electronic gadgets
but the clock and fax machine remained his most
important contributions to modern life. There is a
monument to him at the village hall, where the
inscription refers to the fax machine as 'The Electric
Printing Telegraph'.

As the list of local saints suggests, Watten was
an important centre long before electricity had been
discovered. Lying on the shore of the largest loch in

Caithness and on a route from the coast to all points south, it has always been a crossroads and overnight resting place for travellers. To see a map showing the early chapel sites around Watten, turn left at the crossroads as you enter the village and walk along to the garage. Turn in behind the hedge and you will find two flagstone plinths with information panels. One is on the prisoner-of-war camp and the other is on the saints and chapel sites. For those who do not have time for this detour, the map and some of the information is reproduced on the next few pages. More detailed directions can be found in Part Three, Route 6.

The Information Panel at Watten

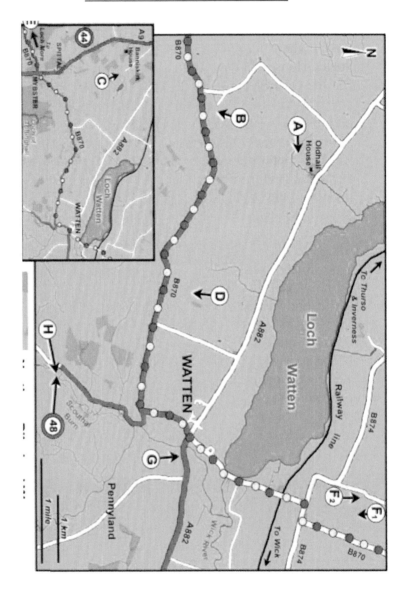

Sites A and B are dedicated to Fumac (6th century), who is associated mainly with Keith in Banffshire. It is thought that St Fumac's Fair was held at Markethill (site B). There are also ruins of a chapel just south of Oldhall House near Dunn (site A). This may have been the Chapel of Dine (or Dunn), which is known locally as the Tomb of Dunn and was dedicated to Fumac.

Sites C and D were dedicated to Magnus (d. 1117AD). Banniskirk (site C) may be a corruption of his name. His fair was formerly held at Wester-Watten (site D) around the time of his feast on 16th April, known in the Middle Ages as Magnusmas. According to some sources, the church in Watten was dedicated to Magnus.[33]

Site E (off the map as it refers to the chapel and holy well already mentioned at Achscoraclete, Loch More which is dedicated to St Bridget (Bridget (c. 451 – 525AD). There are several Bridgets - Brides, Brigits, Bridhdes, some of which are pagan goddesses. Others are cultic goddess/saints and historical figures. The most famous is Bridget of Kildare. There are dedications to Bridget all over Scotland, especially around the Solway, which probably refer to the Irish Bridget. Those in the Highlands and Islands may be referring to a local figure as Bride is a Pictish name (Brude being the male version).

F1 and F2 are dedicated to Katherine of Alexandria (4th Century). The only other well-known Catherine is Catherine of Siena but she belongs to the

---

[33] See Ecclesiastical History of Caithness p.316

14th century, which is too modern for our sites.

Again, we have connections between the local saint, the Sinclair family and Rosslyn Chapel. St Margaret of Scotland (1045-1093) had been given a relic of Katherine. When visiting Rosslyn Castle, she spilt a drop of the oil from this relic into a well on the grounds. The water from this well then developed healing powers and the Sinclair family, owners of the castle, adopted Katherine as their patron saint. There is a legend of William St Clair of Rosslyn, at the time of Robert the Bruce (1274-1329), who prayed to St Katherine to help him to catch a white deer before it escaped across a river as its escape would mean his death. A hound appeared and turned the deer back. William later built a chapel to the south of Edinburgh dedicated to her. The site at Watten dedicated to Katherine consisted of a chapel, holy well and monastery/ nunnery on the outskirts of the village past the Church of Scotland manse. For details of other sites in Caithness dedicated to Katherine, see the Alphabetical List of Saints in Part Four under Catherine/Katherine.

Site G at Torr Tharlogain (Tarlogan's Hill) is dedicated to Tarlogan / Talorcan (7 th century) (also referred to as: Talarican, Talorgan, Tarquin, Tarloc, Tarlork, Tarloga, and Tarkin). Tarlogan was a common Pictish name. He was a follower of Donan and was with him on the Isle of Eigg. He is said to have been ordained by Pope Gregory[34]. In Caithness,

---

[34] Probably Pope Gregory I who encouraged the evangelisation of Europe and sent Augustine to England as bishop of Canterbury.

he is remembered here and at Tarlogan's church (Teampull Tharlogain) in Halkirk. This site is easily identified as it is shared with the ruined Church of Scotland, across the river from Braal Castle.

Site H at Scouthal Burn is dedicated to Mary (1st century). Dedications to Mary, the mother of Jesus, multiplied after the 12th century, sometimes replacing older ones. Sites include the chapel, well and burial place at The Clow on Scouthal Burn. For long after the Reformation, people would visit this chapel on the first Sunday after the new moon. The Marymas Fair, held in Dunnet in August, suggests a dedication to Mary in the area. Another ancient site dedicated to Mary is Marykirk of Sibster, near Wick.

Site no 44 is Spittal on the Northern Saints' Trails route 6

Site no 48 is Scouthal Burn, also on the Northern Saints' Trails route 6

Pennyland is an area south-east of the village centre. Its name suggests that it was once owned by the church. However the Northern Pilgrims' Way stays closer to the loch as it moves on to the next site.

On the way to Canisbay, the minor road from the turn-off at Hastigrow passes two sites of relevance to us. The first is Chapel Field at Lyth (ND 2909 6220), just to the east of Barrock House, as the field is said to have been the site of a chapel dedicated to Finbarr (or Bar, as it is called locally). Further along the road is Brabster. Beside Brabstermire House is the site of a chapel and graveyard dedicated to Tustan/Drostan (ND 3170 6937). The baptismal font from the chapel was kept in Brabstermire House.

Canisbay

Saint: Drostan (see also Trothan/Trostan/Tear/Teer)
(6th Century)   site no 14 on the NST

This is the last of our NPW sites on the mainland of
Scotland.

The modern parish church stands on the main
road between Thurso and John O'Groats. It is best
known today as the place of worship for the royal
family when they stay at the near-by Castle of May.
The current building has a long history, going back to
the 15th Century, and some of the stonework may even
go back to the 13th century but our interest in it lies in
the ruins between this building and the shore which
mark the site of a chapel dedicated to Drostan, or
Trostan as he was known in Caithness. This was
known as 'the Kirk by the Sea'. At low tide, a rock in
line with this ruin can be seen and is known as 'the
papel rock'.[35]

Gills Bay and on to Kirkwall

To the west of Canisbay is the modern ferry terminal
of Gills Bay. It is operated by Pentland Ferries, who
run a car and foot passenger ferry all year round (with
the exception of a few public holidays and times when
weather conditions make it unsafe). The journey takes
apr one hour and terminates at St Margaret's Hope.
There is normally a bus waiting to take passengers on

---

[35] See paparproject.org.uk/caithness1.html for further details

to Kirkwall but be warned that, if the ferry is running late, the bus does not wait for it!

It is not clear which Margaret the Hope is named after. One possibility is the Maid of Norway, mentioned earlier, but she is not on the official Calendar of Saints. A more likely candidate is Saint Margaret, joint patron saint of Scotland with St Andrew and wife of King Malcolm Canmore.

While pilgrimages are traditionally made on foot, I suggest here that the pilgrim takes the bus from St Margaret's Hope into Kirkwall instead as the journey includes several causeways linking the islands that make up Orkney. These causeways do not have pedestrian walkways and can be quite busy. You will still have to walk the last small section from the bus centre to the cathedral, the end/starting point of the NPW.

Another option is the Scrabster to Stromness ferry, run by NorthLink Ferries. This would allow the pilgrim to join the St Magnus Way[36] which traces the journey taken by the corpse of St Magnus from the spot where he was murdered on the island of Egilsay to the cathedral in Kirkwall. This route can be joined at either Finstown or Orphir by either:
a) walk/take the Kirkwall bus to Finstown and walk along the Way from there. It is apr 7.2 miles from Stromness to Finstown and another 7 miles from there to Kirkwall

---

[36] For details of the St Magnus Way, go to www.stmagnusway.com.

b) walk/take the bus to the Loch of Stenness, walk along the minor road through Stenness and Houton to Orphir and walk along the Way from there. It is apr 8.5 miles from Stromness to Orphir and apr 11.5 miles from there to Kirkwall.

For both options, you are advised to have a map of Orkney and check the official guide to the St Magnus Way.

A third option is the passenger ferry from John O'Groats to Burwick on the most southerly point of Orkney (this operates in the summer only, so please check in advance). A bus takes passengers from the ferry into Kirkwall. For pilgrims with more time to spare, there are various possible walking routes between the ferry and the first causeway (check these at https://www.orkney.gov.uk/Service-Directory/C/Core-Paths.html and search for South Ronaldsay).For an extensive list of ancient chapel sites in the area, go to http://www.paparproject.org.uk/orkney4.html.

Whatever option the pilgrim uses to travel through Orkney, the final destination is always St Magnus' Cathedral. This is the most northerly cathedral in Britain. It is currently used as the Church of Scotland parish church for Kirkwall but belongs to the whole community. It was built by the nephew of the martyred Magnus, Rognvald, as a suitable repository for his uncle's relics. These relics were moved, with permission from the bishop, from Birsay to within a pillar of the cathedral. This was the final signal that Magnus had been officially recognised as a saint. When Rognvald was himself murdered while on a hunting trip in Caithness, his body was taken to the cathedral and is also buried there. Rognvald was later declared a saint.

The cathedral is normally open to the public and guided tours can be arranged. It was a wonderful achievement for its day and rightly deserves the title of 'Light of the North'. More details can be found at www.Stmagnus.org.

So ends the journey of between 115 and 120 miles, depending on which braid has been followed. Hopefully, it marks the beginning of a new journey of self-discovery, peace of mind and a renewed sense of connection with nature and those who went before us.

Now we need to return to Helmsdale and join those pilgrims who have decided to take Braid Two. They stay on the John O'Groats Trail through Helmsdale and on to Dunbeath.

Following Braid Two

Just north of Helmsdale is Navidale, an area associated with Ninian. Saint Ninian's chapel, well and graveyard are at ND 0407 1625 but nothing can now be seen. It is said that the original chapel was burned down by the Mackays in a clan feud in 1556. A Celtic carved stone was found at the site and is now in the Dunrobin Museum. St Ninian's Bay can be accessed by a path from the road – ask locally for exact directions.

About 2.5 miles from Helmsdale is the gorge known as the 'Ord of Caithness'. This marks the boundary between Sutherland and Caithness. Caithnesians still refer to 'going over the Ord' when travelling south. There is no record of early chapel sites here and the only religious connection seems to be the story connected to the long struggle between the followers of Charles I and Charles II, who were trying to impose an episcopal form of church governance in Scotland, and the Covenanters who supported a form similar to that of the present Church of Scotland. An important figure in this struggle was James Graham, 1st Marquess of Montrose. The story is complicated and the only part that is relevant here is Montrose's return from exile in Norway in 1650, when he arrived via Orkney. On Orkney, he recruited a small army. He sent some of them ahead to secure the Ord crossing and they camped overnight at the side of the burn.

Having crossed the Ord River, the next point of interest is the Ousdale Broch. This is one of the best-preserved brochs in Caithness and has recently had much work done on it to make it accessible to visitors. For details, go to www.thebrochproject.co.uk. There are no chapel sites listed here but there are records of a medieval hospital/hostel near the current Ousdale farm, suggesting that travellers regularly passed this spot. It is also thought to have been used as a camp site by King William and his army in 1201, when they came north to avenge the mutilation of Bishop John by Earl Harold of Orkney – see 'A tale of Two Bishops' above.

The NPW guidebook now suggests a short deviation from the JOGT to avoid a very steep descent to the bottom of the gorge. By following the track created by the Caithness Broch Project group, the pilgrim can walk along the edge of the A9 (not pleasant but there is a reasonable verge) to the car park created for visitors to the remains of the Badbea clearance village. This village was home to a group of about fifteen families who had been cleared from their crofts to this cliff-top site in the late 1700's. It is said that small children had to be tethered to posts to prevent them falling over the cliff to their deaths. Most of the families emigrated to New Zealand.

Just past Badbea is another gorge - Berriedale. The modern Berriedale is famous for the steep gradient of the main road, recently improved on the north side but still warranting escape beds on the south side for vehicles that end up going down the slope rather faster than intended.[37] The name comes from Saint

---

[37] If you are a car-driver, please only use these in a real emergency as they can cause serious damage to the underside of the car!

Finbar, who was born in the area. This is the same Finbar as was mentioned with regard to Dornoch Cathedral. A short distance up the Langwell River (south of the Berriedale Water, which it joins at the road bridge) is a hillside known as Cnoc Fionn or Cadha Fhionn, presumed to be the place of his birth. It now only has a few ruined buildings to mark the spot. Slightly further up on the same side of the river is a chapel site, Brae na h- eaglaise, the hill of the church. A hill with the same name is on the opposite side of the river.

Another site whose name is said to derive from Finbar is Achvarasdale on the Thurso to Reay road. There is another broch here that has been cleared of weeds by the CBP group.

Having negotiated Berriedale, the JOGT follows the cliff-tops for apr 6 miles before turning inland to Dunbeath. For those pilgrims following Braid Two, the route turns inland just to the south of the village where the road to Braemore branches off from the A9. Hopefully, those pilgrims will have time to explore Dunbeath before moving inland.

Dunbeath

Dunbeath is best known as the birth place of the novelist, Neil Gunn. There is a sculpture of one of his best-known characters, 'Ken', at the harbour. More about him and the wider history of the area can be found at the excellent Dunbeath Heritage Museum.

There was a large early monastic settlement, the House of Peace or Chapel Hill, just up the river bank from the village at Ballachly, which was used as a hostel for both religious and civic travellers. Some sources say that the House of Peace was dedicated to St Triduana but this might be caused by confusion with the Caithness site, also at a place called Ballachly. On the other hand, with Kintradwell a day's walk away, it could be correct. An incised cross slab was found at Ballachly Farm. It is now in the Dunbeath Heritage Museum. For a picture and details of the site, see https://www.dunbeath-heritage.org.uk/4-chapel-hill-ballachly

Further up the riverside path is one of several brochs in the area. A bridge over the river leads to a path that joins the road from Dunbeath to Braemore. In theory, this would make an attractive circular walk. However parts of the path past the House of Peace are overgrown with bracken, making walking difficult.

Not far from the village towards the north on the A9 is the Laidhay Croft Museum and tea-room which gives an insight into life in the area in the 19th and 20th Centuries. This is a bit off our route but worth a visit for those who can stay in the area for a day or two.

Having explored Dunbeath, the pilgrim on Braid Two has to back-track to the Braemore road junction and take this side-road to the next place of interest.

Braemore to Loch More

Saint: Ciaran

The end of the public road is marked by a red phone box. This is one of the few traditional phone boxes still in operation as it provides an essential line for the emergency services.[38] From here to the other side of Loch More, internet signals cannot be relied on. If the pilgrim is using a form of sat nav on their mobile phones, they need to be sure to download that day's details onto the phone the night before, make sure that the phone is fully charged and carry a back-up battery charger with them. In addition to all that, a good old-fashioned OS map and compass are recommended.

There is a ruin here knows as 'An Abaide' or 'the abbot's house' which has been provisionally dated to the late 11th century. Elderly residents of Dunbeath can confirm the name and have memories of playing in the ruins. It is on the opposite side of the river to the phone box and slightly closer to the village (ND 0794 2962). On the same side of the river as the abbot's house but closer to the phone box and beside Braemore Lodge is the site of a chapel and graveyard (ND 0673 3043). The graveyard contains the ruins of a family mausoleum, bearing the inscription 'rebuilt in 1844'.

Having the abbot's house separate from the chapel and graveyard is a sign of a fairly large

---

[38] Information correct at time of writing but BT make regular attempts to disconnect this phone and sell the box, so please check.

community. This suggests that Braemore was an important monastic settlement and the site was a regular overnight resting place for travellers.

We are now on the 'old road to Thurso' (see the map of core paths on the Scotways website https://www.scotways.com and look for the menu 'Heritage Paths'). The next settlement on this path is Glutt, two miles along from Braemore. Near Glutt Lodge, on the south side of the river are the remains of a small building, thought to be a chapel site (NC 999 368).

Continuing in a northerly direction, follow the Glutt Water to Dalgannachan, where the Rumsdale Water becomes the River Thurso. Closer to the head of the Rumsdale Water is the remains of a sheepfold which is said to have been built from the stones of a chapel dedicated to St Cieran. St Ciaran is associated with the area between the head of Rumsdale Water and Latheron. He has another dedication at the next point on our route, Dalnawillan. The lodge, now unused, was the main seat of the Sinclair family who have owned the estate for centuries. There is an ancient graveyard further up the hill associated with St Ciaran.

The River Thurso now leads us to the shore of Loch More, where we deviate from the Old Road to Thurso at Dalnaha by continuing along the westerly shore to join Route One at the northerly shore of the loch. Earlier travellers would have forded the River Thurso at Dalnaha and followed the southerly bank of Loch More, passing Achscoraclate and St Bridget's chapel and well. All that is left of the chapel is a grassy mound but the well can still be seen. There is a clear path from the public road at the east side of the loch to Ascoraclate, so walkers can visit the site from that end. This would add approximately 5 miles (8km) to that day's walk. The original pilgrims would have stayed to the south of the River Thurso and forded it at either Acharynie graveyard, just past Strathmore Lodge, or at the older fording point between Dirlot Castle (now ruined) and Dirlot graveyard. The Acharynie crossing was used by the cattle drovers of the 18th century as the Dirlot ford is at a gorge which cattle could not negotiate. It is possible that the modern walker, already on the tar road, could access the Dirlot graveyard by following the river from Acharynie. They would pass some standing stones but they might also have to climb a fence. To date, this route has not been tested. The graveyard is also described earlier as we are now on the combined Braids One and Two. So it is time to return to Dunbeath and meet up with those pilgrims who have decided to stay by the coast and continue on the JOGT.

Following Braid Three

From Dunbeath to the end of the road, the countryside has too many archaeological remains in the shape of brochs, cairns, standing stones, carved stones and others to be able to mention them all. Do have a look at the Highland Environmental Record map for details.

The first stop should be the Laidhay Croft Museum and Teahouse but this would mean a detour from the JOGT, which stays close to the shore at this point. So the next point of interest is Latheron.

Latheron

Saint: Ciaran   site no 22 on the NST

Just before the village and half-way between the road and the shore is a chapel site (ND 1982 3301). This seems to have been a fairly large building and local tradition says that it was a hostel. On the other side of the burn is the Clan Gunn Museum, housed in the former Church of Scotland parish church. This was built in 1734 but includes features from a much earlier building and is thought to be on the site of a chapel dedicated to Ciaran. The museum is worth the short detour from the JOGT but do check that it is open as it is run by volunteers.

The JOGT continues to Lybster.

Lybster

Saints: Martin; Mary   site no 21 on the NST

Lybster was begun as a planned village in 1802 by the local landowner, General Patrick Sinclair. His sons fought at the Battle of Waterloo in 1815 and in their honour he named the section of Main Street, where it met what is now the A99, 'Quatre Bras', the village where a British army were victorious over the French in a rehearsal for the more famous battle of Waterloo.

A side-road leads down to the harbour. It passes a waterfall. Between the waterfall and the road is the site of a chapel dedicated to Mary. Close by, but on the other side of the road, is the 'Well of the Brethren', thought to be referring to Sts Peter and Andrew. It was near here that the Lybster Stone was found. This is a large boulder with a simple cross engraved on it. It has a natural bowl-shaped indentation, suggesting that it was chosen for use as a baptismal font. It is now under a flagstone shelter at the local Church of Scotland building (ND 2479 3564).

There is a museum and café at the harbour – Waterlines – which is well worth a visit.

The JOGT now follows the cliff-tops towards Whaligoe, passing. through Mid-Clyth, where there is a graveyard and cross-slab to be seen (ND 2954 3722). There was also a chapel at the graveyard whose remains were still visible in the late 1800's but which had disappeared by the 1900's.

Whaligoe

There are no recorded religious sites at Whaligoe and the name is usually taken to be 'whale's geo'. The geo, with its narrow entrance and steep cliffs giving shelter for the small bay, could have been used for trapping and killing whales. It was certainly used for landing catches from the fishing boats during the herring boom of the late 1800s. The extremely long and steep stone steps were constructed so that fisherwomen could carry these catches in creels on their back up to the road.

Despite the lack of any written records, there is a local tradition that a holy woman lived at the beach and that the geo has the feel of a holy place.

The JOGT continues up the coast. A short distance inland from the trail at Ulbster is a graveyard and mausoleum. The mausoleum is on the site of a chapel dedicated to St Martin. It has a weather vane on the roof with the date '1700' on it. A corner of the surrounding graveyard was the original setting of the carved cross known as the Ulbster Stone, the inspiration for the NPW logo. This is currently in the North Coast Visitors Centre, Thurso. See https://highlandpictishtrail.co.uk/project/north-coast-visitor-centre/ for details.

From Ulbster, the JOGT continues into the town of Wick.

Wick

Saints: Fergus; Francis, Ninian   site no 19 on the NST

Wick has been a Royal Borough since 1589 and is the administrative centre of Caithness. The name of the town comes from the Norse 'Vic, meaning a bay.

During the 19th century, Wick was an important herring fishing port and for a time was the busiest such port in the country, partly due to the harbour redesigned by Thomas Telford, who also designed the southern part of the town known as Pultneytown. The herring trade only lasted for three to four months in the summer and was supported by large numbers of migrant workers, many from the west coast and outer islands. This is where the link with religion comes in as these workers were predominantly Roman Catholic in an area where this denomination had been almost completely wiped out at the Reformation. So the Catholic hierarchy sent a priest to Wick just for the herring season. Then there was a plague epidemic in 1832 and everyone that could, left the town for safer parts. However the priest, Fr Walter Lovi, stayed to care for the sick. In thanks, the town council gifted a plot of land to the Church for a church site. So St Joachim's was built and is still in use today. For much of the 19th Century, the parish was classed as part of the Mission to the Artic. The church's name was decided by one of the early priests, who had a devotion to Jesus' maternal grandfather, Joachim.

The main parish church of Wick is named after the patron saint of Wick, Fergus. There is some dispute over which St Fergus is referred to here. In the 6th century, St Drostan came to the county with three companions, Fergus, Modan (or Medan) and Colm. Then a Fergus voted for the reforms debated at the Synod of Whitby in 664 and a Bishop Fergus attended a council in Rome in 721. However Drostan and his three have many dedications in the county, signifying a powerful influence and many followers, so the dedication of Wick to the earliest Fergus is the most likely answer. A site at what is now called Mount Hooly Terrace at the top of Shore Road in the town is believed to be Fergus' cell. A later chapel dedicated to Fergus existed in what is now the Sinclair Aisle beside the current St Fergus Church. The Mount Hooly site is also linked with a convent dedicated to St Francis. Some sources give 'Cloister' as the name of the site.

Medieval Wick had an effigy of Fergus, which was much venerated. This was destroyed in 1613 by a local minister, the Rev Dr Richard Merchiston of Bower, who was determined to remove all traces of 'popish' practices. The locals were so incensed by this that they waylaid the minister, threw him into the river and watched him drown. They then spread the story that it had been St Fergus himself who had, not just thrown the minister in, but had then sat on him until he drowned. A replacement effigy was made and spent some time in the Sinclair Aisle of the medieval church (the gable end of which can still be seen in the grounds of the present church). It was then moved to the local museum. When this closed down, it was re-located to the St Fergus Church where it is beautifully mounted in front of a stained -glass window. The figure is dressed in monk's robes with the hair cut in the shape of the Roman tonsure. There is a carved heraldic *lion couchant* at his feet. The shape suggest that the effigy was used as a grave slab or sarcophagus top. A (minority) local opinion is that the presence of the heraldic 'wee dug' suggests that this effigy does not represent Fergus but a clerical member of the Sinclair family, after whom the Sinclair Aisle is named. This would be a better match for the suggested date of the effigy (late 15th or early 16th Century), than the 'replacement effigy' theory which would have to be post-1613. At one point, the effigy had an elaborate carved wooden surround but this has disappeared. A baptismal font from the original St Fergus Chapel was found in the Free Church Manse garden in 1840 and was later used as an animal drinking bowl. Marks on the rim suggest that it was also used to sharpen knives. It is now in the present-day St Fergus Church. A 'Fergus Fair' was held in Wick on the fourth Tuesday of November.

Modern visitors to Wick will find much of interest in the Wick Heritage Museum, close to the harbour. If they then go up to the top of the street, they can walk along the shortest street in the world, Ebeneezer Street, which runs along the gable end of the Mackay's Hotel. Wick also hosts its own distillery, producing the 'Old Pulteney' single malt. Sir William Pulteney, governor of the British Fisheries Society, commissioned Thomas Telford in 1786 to build work areas and housing for those involved in the fishing trade, so the area was named after him.

The pilgrim now follows the coast northwards, going through the small villages of Papigoe and Staxigoe. Between the road and the cliff (ND 3844 5163) is a site thought to be that of a chapel dedicated to Ninian. Some old maps name the location of the current lighthouse on the South Pier at the harbour as 'St Ninian's Point' (ND 3707 5061) but the name 'Papigoe' suggests a religious site.[39] Also, Papigoe and Staxigoe had small but sheltered harbours, more suited to small boats than the more exposed Wick harbour before it was modernised.

Wick is the third site dedicated to Ninian that we have met on the coast, suggesting a group of his supporters gradually moving further and further north. See the entry '18. Papigoe' in the section Route 5 of Part Three for further details.

---

[39] See paparproject.org.uk/caithness2.html for further details

Ackergill

Saint: Drostan   site no 17 on the NST

The next site of interest is just past Castles Sinclair and Girnigoe at an area known as Shorelands, Ackergill (ND 3672 5448). Here there is a small cairn, erected by the Clan Gunn Society in 1999, marking the site of St Tear's Chapel. This is one of the better-known ancient chapel sites as it is linked to a feud between the Clan Gunn and the Clan Mackay. Representatives of each side agreed to meet in the chapel to discuss a peace settlement but the MacKays brought twice as many men as had been agreed and killed the Gunns.

I repeat here a summary from various sources on this site. (Bishop Forbes, quoted below, visited the site in 1762). On the debate about the dedication to Tear, the modern consensus is that this is a form of Drostan, who was known as Trostan in Caithness. Substituting T for D is a feature of Old Welsh, which was probably very similar to the language spoken by Drostan and his followers. Drostan was a founder of the community at Deer in Buchan that produced the Book of Deer, so it is not surprising that one variant of his name was Tear (others were Trostan, Tristan, Tustan and Trothan).

Information on the Chapel Site at Ackergill

Rev D. Beaton 'Ecclesiastical History of Caithness and Annals of Caithness Parishes (pub. 1909)

The following extract is from pp51-52 of Chapter IV. (The punctuation is as in the original)

'At some distance from Ackergill, on the farm of Shorelands, can still be seen the spot where stood the old chapel of St Tears (Tayr, Tay, Ere, Aire). ... The lines of the foundation are very clearly marked, and can be easily traced. The chapel was evidently of the larger type of such buildings found in Caithness. It appears to mark the foundation of a chapel by one of the early Celtic missionaries, Drostan by name,[40] whose missionary labours in Caithness are commemorated in a number of chapels. ... Bishop Forbes gives the following interesting account of the Chapel and some of the superstitious practices connected with it: – "Up the shore", he says "a mile from Ackergill, and near the point of Noss Head, are the old castles of Sinclair and Girnigoe, to view which I walked with Wester before Dinner. About a third of the way we came to the ruins of a very singular little Chapel of stone and mortar, without any Lime, and without Windows either in the East or West Gable, all the windows being in the South Wall. It is called the Chapel of St Tear, and the country people, to this very day, assemble here in the morning of the Feast of the

---

[40] See chapter V. and Appendix I. for an explanation of the way the name *Drostan* probably came to be transformed into *Tear*, and for a brief account of Drostan.

Holy Innocents and say their Prayers, bringing their Offerings along with them, some Bread, others Bread and Cheese, others Money etc., and putting these into the Holes of the Walls. In the afternoon they get music – a Piper and Fiddler – and dance on the Green where the Chapel stands. The roof is off, but the walls are almost all entire. One of the late presbyterian preachers of Wick thought to have abolished this old practice; and for that end appointed a diet of catechising in that corner of the parish upon the day of the Holy Innocents, but no one attended him; all went, as usual, to St Tear's Chapel. I saw the font-Stone for Baptism lying on the Green at the East End of the Chapel. Mr Sutherland, of Wester, observed that no doubt it had been called the Chapel of St Tear from the Tears of the Parents and other Relations of the murdered Innocents"[41] Rev. Charles Thomson, writing in 1840, says: – Within the memory of persons yet living, it was customary for people to visit the chapel of St Tear on Innocents' Day, and leave in it bread and cheese, as an offering to the souls of the children slain by Herod; but which the dog-keeper of a neighbouring gentleman used to take out and give to the hounds."[42]'

Chapter V pp.82-83
'Among the Celtic Church missionaries who laboured in Caithness, none has left his name commemorated in so many chapels as Drostan. The name appears in

---

[41] Journals p.211
[42] New Stat. Account (Caithness), p.161

various forms, such as Trostan, Tristan, Tustan, Trothan and Tear or Tears, which again has many variants.'

Appendix I
'Drostan appeared in Caithness prior to Donnan's advent. Meantime we need not dwell on Drostan's connection with Deer but give Mr Scott's[43] explanation of the transmutation of the name Drostan into Tayre or Tears as we have at Ackergill. "When we link up" he says "the Tears legend of Drostan's Church at Westfield, the name of this church at Ackergill, and the legend of S. Drostan's 'tears' in the Book of Deer we feel that there must be some rational explanation of the repeated association of Tears with the saint's name. What is it? *Drost* or *Drust* in the Celtic spoken by the Picts means *dear*. But the meaning of Drust became very debased; and there is another Celtic word *daor* which means *dear*. Is it possible that out of pure delicacy the Celtic converts interchanged *Daor* for Drust and spoke of Drostan as S. Daor or S. Taor which would account for the Caithness 'Tayre'; and that later Celts, like the Gaelic scribe in the Book of Deer misled by pronunciation or spelling or folk-etymology, conceived that *Daor* was *Dear*, which means *Tear*."'

Third Report and Inventory of the Monuments and Constructions in the County of Caithness by the Royal Commission on the Ancient and Historical

---

[43] The author is referring to Rev A.B. Scott, quoted elsewhere.

monuments and Constructions of Scotland. (pub 1911)

595. St Tear's Chapel, Shorelands – the report repeats Bishop Forbes' details, as quoted in Beaton. It adds the following comments on the dedication:

'The dedication of this chapel is a source of much speculation. It is given as St Tear's, St Tayre, St Tay or St Ere and is said to refer to the Holy Innocents. It is possibly a dedication transferred in Roman Catholic times from an earlier Celtic dedication to St Airerain or Ereran, whose day is given in the Irish missal preserved at Drummond Castle as 29th December, one day after that of the Holy Innocents.'

It is time to move on! Following the shore round Sinclair Bay and past Ackergill Tower, there is a very early burial site. This has been excavated. (See ND 3486 5497 on the HER map.). Parts of two symbol stones have been found and are now in the National Museum of Scotland. There are no indications that this was a Christian site.

Further on at Birkle Hill is the site of another symbol stone. The site must have been a food-gatherers encampment as there is a shell-midden. (See ND 3391 5847 on the HER map.) Again, there are no signs of Christian influence. So we can move on through the village of Keiss. Just north of Keiss at the side of the road is a site known as Kirk Tofts with a broch and graveyard. There is a rectangular foundation between the graveyard and the road that might have been the chapel site. Others think that the chapel was in the graveyard and yet others deny any evidence, archaeological or folklore, of a chapel.

The next small village is Auckengill, which has an interesting village hall, 'St Clare's Hall'. The name may refer to the local Sinclair family, rather than be a direct reference to the saint.

Freswick
Saint: Modan/ Maden/Medan   ite no 16 on the NST

Freswick Bay lies between steep cliffs, making it a natural shelter for small boats. Today, the bay is dominated by Freswick Castle but it has sheltered humans since the Iron Age. The shore hides the oldest known Viking settlement in Scotland and there are several brochs near-by. So it is no surprise that it is associated with a chapel and graveyard dedicated to one of 'Drostan's Three' –Modan (or Medan). The Madan associated with Bowermadden (ND 262 648) may be a different person. Local people would visit the chapel on Candlemas Day, which was close to the feast day of Modan on Feb 4th. See the Alphabetical List for more details. The chapel fell into ruins after the Reformation and a mausoleum was built on the site by Sir William Sinclair around 1670. This itself is now in a ruinous state, although the unusual round windows can still be seen. It can be approached by a stone bridge over the burn at the north side of Freswick Castle.

The route continues along the cliff tops to Duncansby Head, Sannick Bay and John O'Groats.

John O'Groats

Saint; Mary   site no 15 on the NST

Just before the village there is a small burn, then a slight grassy mound, then a swing gate. The grassy mound (ND 3867 7347) is all that remains of Saint Mary's Chapel, or the Lady Kirk as it is known locally. This may be a re-dedication as the site so close to the shore suggests a dedication to one of the early Celtic saints. It seems to have been in use into the 14th century as a hoard of silver coins from the reigns of five kings was found there in 1969. The kings ranged from Henry III (1216-72) and Alexander III to Robert I (1306-29) and Edward II (1307-27), but most were from the time of Edward I (1272 -1307). Some of them are in the National Museum of Scotland, a few are in the Wick Museum.

John O'Groats itself is named after the Dutchman, Jan de Groot who was given the franchise by King James IV to run a ferry service between there and Orkney. He did much to develop the area, for long erroneously thought to be Britain's most northerly point (which is actually Dunnet Head). His gravestone can be seen in Canisbay Church, just along the coast. John O' Groats is still thought of as 'the end of the road' and the ferry still runs, but in summertime only. Between John O Groats and Canisbay is the small harbour of Huna. Local tradition says that this was the most popular harbour for traffic between Orkney and Caithness in the days of small sailing boats

Canisbay

See under Braid One.

Gills Bay and on to Kirkwall

See under Braid One.

To end this description of the pilgrimage route, the next page has a poem about Duthac and Magnus, composed for a NPW event in Kirkwall on the feast day of Magnus' nephew, Rognvald, on 20th August 2021

St Magnus'Cathedral Kirkwall

Duthac and Magnus [44]

Brave pilgrims all the way from Tain
We hail your Northern Way
How good it is to greet you here
On this, St. Rognvald's day.

The ties between our Kirks and Saints
Go back a thousand year
With hundred miles of track and moor
And boat to persevere.

A Way that pilgrims walked of old
In mediaeval times
For healing, or repentance for
Their sins, misdeeds or crimes.

They were the tourists of the day
Like now, we want them here
They'd need a bed and food and drink
And buy a souvenir.
You speak of Duthac, Man of Tain
An old and worthy Saint
A name that we in Orkney here
Are fairly well acquaint.

When Rognvald built his famous Kirk
That bore his uncle's name
A dedicated shrine therein
Confirmed St. Duthac's fame.

[44] Written by Harvey Johnson for the NPW event in the East Church, Kirkwall, 20th August 2021. Used with permission.

The Sandwick farm of Doehouse had
A stipend to provide
And's noted down as Duthushoose
In 1595.

When Duthac walked up on this earth
And preached and healed round Tain
The North was ruled from Birsay
During great Earl Thorfinn's reign.

They both died in 1065
And though both idolised
An incorrupted body led
To Duthac canonised.

His shrine became a Mecca for
The great men of the day
Where Rob the Bruce would bend his knee
And James the Fourth would pray

Through time the cult of Magnus grew
Killed young, and loved to bits
He had better social media and
Had far more likes and hits.
But we're not in competition
Pilgrims Ways are all the rage
Let's promote religious tourists
In this brand-new Pilgrim-age.

Your Northern Pilgrim Way is good
For body and for mind
Let Magnus and St. Duthac show
A Way for folk to find.

PART THREE: Going Round in Circles

And passing along by the Sea of Galilee, he saw Simon and Andrew the brother of Simon casting a net in the sea; for they were fishermen. And Jesus said to them, 'Follow me and I will make you become fishers of men. And immediately they left their nets and followed him' (Mark 1:16-18).

In this section, I go back several centuries before Duthac and Magnus to the beginnings of Christianity in the north of Scotland. It is this history that most appealed to me when researching the Celtic saints of the north. Long ago, when I first came to live in Caithness and travelled south to visit relatives, I regularly drove along that stretch of the A9 known as the Causwaymyre. This road runs along the edge of a wide expanse of moorland stretching for many miles inland to the mountains of Morven and Scaraben. I always had the urge to abandon the car and just set off into the distance, using these peaks as guides. As I usually had several children in the car, I never gave in to this urge! It was with delight that I discovered that my impulse was not as mad as it had seemed but was an echo of journeys made by many, many people over the centuries. Before the days of roads, people did indeed use these two mountain peaks as guides across the moors.

I felt two other links with these early travellers – my faith comes directly from Saint Columba and his followers as I was brought up in a remote peninsula on the west coast that was by-passed by the Reformation. All the local people were Catholics and owed their faith to missionaries of the same order as those travelling around Caithness. My upbringing was also not dissimilar to that of the people whom the missionaries served – no proper roads, no electricity, water from wells and burns. As few other people share this background, the following sections are designed to help the reader get a feel for life in the first centuries AD in Caithness.

An Overview of the Political/Religious Scene.

I am grateful to John Williams, a founder member of the NST group, for the following overview:

SCOPE: These notes are intended only to outline some people and events contemporary with those mentioned in the "NORTHERN SAINTS TRAILS" leaflet produced by Caithness Book Club in 2018. It follows that the times mentioned are from the 1st century A.D. to just after the death of Gilbert-of-Caithness in 1245. The geographical scope is also restricted to the parts of what are currently called Caithness and Sutherland, Scotland, England and Christendom. Borders of Counties, Earldoms, and the concept of nationalities have to be thought of in terms of the situation at the time under consideration.

CAUTION ABOUT NAMES, LANGUAGES AND SOURCES: To write of a country called 'Scotland' in a language called 'English' would have mystified most residents of the 1st to 14th centuries. Scotland as a Kingdom started, perhaps, to have meaning in 843 A.D.: England in the language we use, even later. The Northern Saints would have recognised the letters of the text you are reading now in the Roman alphabet, but they would have understood Aramaic or Brythonic, Gaelic, Norse, Norn, Old Welsh and Latin; possibly Koin Greek too; but no modern English at all: for most of us the English of Bede in the 8th century is unintelligible, that of Chaucer in the 14th difficult. Similarly, we have to treat even the best, or often the only, stories of the early Saints with caution: fireside tales from oral tradition, told for moral purposes, rather than as cross-referenced histories.

1st to 3rd centuries: The Blessed Virgin Mary, John the Baptist, Peter.

Pictland-Caithness
Broch-building ends before c.200AD.
Pictland-Scotland
Pictish Iron-age continues to flourish north of the walls

Britania Romana
- Southern Britain invaded successfully in 43AD by the Roman Empire under Claudius.
- Romanisation of elites continued throughout these centuries.

- Use of Latin & the Roman alphabet becomes widespread.
- Troubles caused by marauding Saxons in the 3rd century - Canterbury's walls built in 270 AD as a countermeasure including a gate giving pedestrian access to what is now St Martin's Church (both the gate & church remain in use in the C.21st.).

Christendom
- The life, death & resurrection of Jesus Christ in Palestine.
- St Peter goes to Rome. Papacy established.
- St Paul & the other Apostles spread Christianity throughout the Roman Empire &Neighbouring lands.
- 29 Popes from St Peter to Marcellinus, d.304.

4th century: Martin-of-Tours, George, Gavin, Katherine, Triduana?

Pictland-Caithness
Pictish language dominant.
Pictland-Scotland
Old Welsh spoken in what is now Strathclyde

Britania Romana
- Britain south of the walls continues a flourishing part of the Roman Empire, exporting grain, livestock, hides, dogs, slaves, tin & precious metals.

- Saxon & other heathen attackers repelled successfully

Christendom
- 11 Popes from Marcellus to Anastasius I.
- The C4th opened with the Emperor Diocletian persecuting Christians & attempting to eradicate the Church but ended with Christianity being, in effect, the state religion of the whole Roman Empire. (Constantine granted freedom of worship to all religions in 313).
- 325 Council of Nicea ended the Arian heresy and introduced the Nicene Creed

5th century:

Pictland-Caithness
Part of a more or less stable established Pictish Kingdom.
Pictland-Scotland
Known Pictish Kings:
Drust I d.478
Tarlogan I d.482.
Succession in Pictland was not necessarily by primogeniture: the next king being chosen from possible male adult contenders only after the death of the incumbent. An interregnum was thus normal.

Britania Romana
410: Withdrawal of the legions from the provinces of Britannia. Start of the post-roman period in Britain

with the breakdown of the cash economy, the end of commercial agriculture with a return to subsistence farming. Trade by barter, wine for slaves. Population crashes, partly due to famines & epidemics & partly due to strife. Loss of perhaps 75% of the population in 2 generations.

Christendom
- 12 Popes from Innocent I to Symmachus, d. 514.
- 400: Pelagius, an English monk, went to Rome preaching the 'Pelagian heresy'.
- 431: Council of Ephesus confirmed the title of Theotokos for Mary
- 451: Council of Chalcedon, where the 'Tome of Leo' confirmed the dual nature of Christ.
- 460 (apr) Patrick goes to Ireland
- 670 Book of Durrow written
- 698 Lindisfarne Gospels written

6ᵗʰ century: Modan-of-Stirling, Ciaran, Colman-of-Dromore, Trostan, Colm-of-Buchan, Fergus Columba-of-Iona.

Pictland-Caithness
Part of the well-established Pictish Kingdom
Pictland-Scotland

Pictish Kings:	Drust IV d.558
Nechtan I d.506	Gartnait I d.565
Drust II d.536	Galantan d.548
Galantan d.548	Drust III d.553
Drust III d.553	Drust IV d.558

Gartnait I d.565
Caitran d.566
Tarlogan II d.577
Drust V d.578

Galan d.580
Brude I d.584
Gartnait II d.599

Post-Roman Southern Britain
Much of the lands that are now England submerged in
inter-tribal Saxon, Anglian, Jutish & Frankish power-
struggles which resolved into a heptarchy of kingdoms:

Kent Northumbria Mercia Sussex Essex Wessex Anglia	Of these 7 Kingdoms, Kent, with Jutish Frankish & other continental influence may have kept some Christian heritage was the least ill-disposed of the 7, Augustine being welcomed & appointed 1 Archbishop of Canterbury in 597.

Christendom
- 14 Popes from Hormisdas to Gregory I d.604
  - aka "Gregory the Great" who sent St Augustine
  to Britain.
- 503: The baptism of Clovis
- 521: St Columba aka Colum Cille aka Columba-
  of-Iona born at Gartan, Co Donegal, Ireland.
- 525: foundation of Monte Casino - the effective
  start of the Benedictine Order which still
  flourishes today & which rule is followed at
  Pluscarden Abbey in Moray to the present time.
- 563: St Columba established the Christian
  community on Iona. Died there in 597 having 1st
  attempted the evangelisation of the Picts at

116

Inverness, then King Aidan of Dalriada.- a then newly established Irish kingdom in Argyll.

- 570 Muhammad born in Mecca

7th century: Cuthbert-of-Lindisfarne, Curitan, Colman-of-Iona

Pictland-Caithness
Continued to be part of the well-established Pictish Kingdom
Pictland-Scotland

Pictish Kings:	Tarlogan IV d.657
Nechtan II d.615	Gartnait IV d.663
Kenneth d.631	Drust VI d.672
Gartnait III d.635	Brude III d.693
Brude II d.641	Taran d.697
Tarlogan III d.653	

<u>Dal Riata-Scotland</u> aka Dalriada

- This Irish Christian Celtic kingdom by now firmly established by the "Scotti" in what is now Argyll. Both Saxon Kings Oswald (now St Oswald) & his brother Oswig were brought up here following the killing of their father, Edwin of Northumbria.
- Adamnon, in his biography of Columba, gives the first written description of Nessie.

Post-Roman Southern Britain

- 603: Augustine of Canterbury did not stand to meet the Welsh Bishops at Aust, so was judged haughty & arrogant: not a fit Christian with whom to agree: the differences were partially resolved at

Whitby 61 years later, but rumble on today whenever disputes over Celtic & Roman rites recur. The irony being that the British tradition derived from Rome too - from the days of Empire - while the rites insisted upon by Augustine reflected more recent Roman practices.

- 604: St Lawrence, d.619, succeeded St Augustine at Canterbury, rode out a pagan backlash & continued dialogue with the Christian Celts while actively promoting Christianity to the Angles & Saxons. In this he was ultimately successful - & is honoured by the English naming Canterbury's cricket ground after him. The most "English" of English honours!

- King Aethelfrith of Northumbria ordered the slaughter of 1200 unarmed Welsh monks to prevent their Prayers affecting the outcome of the Battle of Chester in 615, he won the battle but lost the war: Wales remains a Christian country.

- 627? King Raedwald of East Anglia died - a Christian when convenient to minimise conflict with Aethelberht of Kent - Raedwald was the most likely owner of & corpse in the Sutton Hoo treasure - that most pagan of burials.

- 655: King Penda of Mercia died. The most successful of the pagan saxon kings, he had killed St Oswald in 642. Oswald was succeeded by his brother Oswig as King of Northumbria. Oswig died peacefully, being succeeded by his son Ecgfrith in 670.

- 659: one of the worst of a whole series of bad plague years.
- 664: The synod of Whitby: The Abbess Hilde achieved a degree of success in partially reconciling the British & Anglo-Saxon Christians. King Oswig, aka Oswiu, aka Oswy was the civil power at this synod influential in the decision to adopt modern Roman ways despite his Celtic Christian upbringing in Dalriada.

Christendom
- 20 Popes from Sabinian to Sergius I
- 627: Conversion of Northumbria
- 632: Conversion of East Anglia.
- 636: Byzantines lose Syria to the Arabs
- 638 Moslems capture Jerusalem

8th century: Modan-of-Fraserburgh, Fergus-of-Wick-&-Halkirk

Pictland-Caithness
- Viking incursions brought Sutherland (the "Southern land" - it is when viewed from a ship at sea west of Orkney) into existence.
- Increasing threats to Pictish rule north of Tain.

Pictland-Scotland
- Known Pictish Kings:
  Brude IV d.706   Nechtan III d.732
  Tarlogan V k.750   Oengus d.761
- Aed, King of Scots battled against Kenneth King of Picts in 768.

- Constantine defeated Connall in 789 but avoided taking either the title "King-of-Scots" or "King-of-Picts" but was *de facto* the 1st King of Scotland (albeit temporarily).
- Constantine founded a church at Dunkeld, his brother, another Oengus, founded what was to become St.Andrews.
- The unity between Picts & Scots was (temporarily) broken by Viking killings but achieved again by Kenneth macAlpin in the next century & from whom the founding of modern Scotland is taken.
- 794 Iona sacked for the 1st time.

Southern Britain
- 786 - 802 Beorhtric ruled Wessex, during which time vikings attacked Portland.
- 793: Vikings sack Lindisfarne. (This was their 1st securely dated & documented raid).
- 796: Viking raid on the monastery at Jarrow successfully beaten off.

Christendom
- 13 Popes from John VI to Leo III
- 711 - 716: Arabs conquer Spain.
- c.714: St Willibrord led an unsuccessful Christian mission to Scandinavia.
- 716: Boniface's 1st missionary journey to Frisia.
- 731: Bede completes his "Ecclesiastical History".

- 732: Franks defeat Arabs near Poitiers - loss of Europe to Muslims prevented.
- 751: Pepin crowned King of the Franks by the Pope.
- 754: Papal State established. Boniface killed.
- 771 - 814 Charlemagne King of the Franks. He drives the "Carolingian Renaissance".
- 793: Vikings sack Lindisfarne & go on to disrupt European civilisation for the following 300+ years.
- 795 Book of Durrow moved from Lindisfarne to protect it from Viking raids.
- End of the century: Book of Kells begun on Iona and finished at Kells.

9th century

Pictland-Caithness
- 839: Eoganan, last known King of the Northern Picts was killed fighting Norsemen.
- 866: Invasion by Olaf & Asl.
- c.870: Formal establishment of the Viking earldom of Orkney under Rognvald.
- 891: Death of Earl Sigurd-of-Orkney.
- The Norse Earldom included all of the main island of Britain north of a border from Tain to Kinlochewe.

Pictland-Scotland
- Pictland becomes Scotland, "Alba" a unified kingdom of southern picts & Dalriada scots

from 848 formed of lands south of the norse hegemony & north of Strathclyde & Bernicia. Alba ruled by Kenneth I, Kenneth macAlpin, generally recognised as the 1st King of Scots, he ruled 841 - 859 (last known King of the Picts, Drust VII d. 848) then these Kings of Scots: Donald I r.859 - 863,

- Constantine I r.863 - c.877,
- Aed r.c.877 - 878,

Post-Roman Southern Britain

- The heptarchy in Southern Britain:
- Bernicia, an early english-speaking kingdom included Edinburgh & Newcastle.
- 835: Vikings attack Sheppey in the Kingdom of Kent.
- 871: Alfred "The Great" becomes king of Wessex & ultimately checks the expansion of viking hegemony. Died 899.
- 874: Vikings depose Burgred, king of Mercia.

Christendom

- 20 popes form Stephen IV to John IX
- 800: Charlemagne crowned Holy Roman Emperor.
- 806: A Viking attack on Iona left 68 brothers killed.
- 807: Vikings sack Inishmurray off Connaucht.
- 814: Death of Charlemagne.
- 822: Vikings raid Cork.
- c.825: Vikings settle on the Faroes.

- 829 - 865: Anskar of Bremen partially evangelises Denmark & Sweden with his 1st mission to Sweden 829 - 831.
- 839: Vikings attacked the Picts.
- 845: Vikings sack Paris.
- 848: Vikings captured Bordeaux.

10th Century

Pictland-Caithness
980: Earl Sigurd-the-Stout became ruler of Orkney (until 1014).

Pictland-Scotland
Kings of Scots:
       Constantine II 900 - 943
       Malcolm I 943 - 954
       Indulf 954 - 962
       Dubh 962 - 967
       Culen 967 - 971
       Kenneth II 971 - 995
       Constantine III 995 - 997
       Kenneth III 997 – 1005

Post-Roman Southern Britain
924: Edward-the-Elder of Wessex dies & is succeeded by Athelstan, generally regarded as the 1st King of England

Christendom
- 25 Popes from Benedict IV to Sylvester II.

- 924: Land grants in Normandy increase the size & power of the Viking duchy there.
- 924: The Althing is set up in Iceland.
- 965: Harald-Bluetooth of Denmark converted to Christianity.
- 986: Erik-the-red established a Viking colony in Greenland.
- 988: The Varangian Guard established by Basil II of Byzantium.
- 988: Vladimir of Kiev converted to Christianity.

A more domestic view.

The geography of Caithness is almost uniformly that of a flat area of peat bog resting on sandstone, with spectacular cliffs protecting it from the sea and a ridge of granite mountains marking the border with Sutherland. The sandstone has produced layers of flagstone that are comparatively easy to extract as slabs, used by the locals vertically as an alternative to fences and horizontally as walls for buildings. In more modern times, a thriving flagstone industry developed, exporting the flags as paving for the streets of towns and cities world-wide.

The earliest known buildings were round, with stone and wattle walls and thatched roofs, probably supported by wooden poles fixed into the ground inside the stone wall. By the time of the early saints, buildings were square or rectangular with rafters and thatch. That so many sites are still discernible is due to the excellent quality of the flagstone as a building material.

The county has very few trees but the peat means that it was once heavily forested. One theory for the disappearance of these forests is that they were burned down to reduce the shelter available to predatory animals such as the Caledonian bear and the wolf.

During the 1st and 2nd centuries, the weather became cooler and damper. This affected the amount of food that could be grown in any one area. So the population had to be evenly spread rather than congregating in towns. In Caithness, this pattern can be seen by the distribution of the chapels, holy wells and graveyards. There was some slight clustering in the sheltered, more fertile, straths and at points of arrival/departure by boat but generally the county was fairly evenly populated.

1st to 3rd century

Reindeer, elk, moose, bears, wild pigs, boars, wolves and beavers roam the land. The Caledonian Bear was prized by the Romans and taken to Rome for baiting and torturing prisoners. Bere, an ancient form of barley, is the staple diet in the form of bannocks cooked on girdles.

9th and 10th centuries: Elk, moose and Caledonian bear become extinct.

11th century: Book of Deer written; Macbeth visits Rome in 1050, 10 years into his 17-year reign; in 1070

Malcolm Canmore marries Margaret who invites three Benedictine monks from Canterbury to found a monastery at Dunfermline- the first such establishment in Scotland.

12th century: reindeer and beavers become extinct. Oats now as common as Bere barley. Pope Celestine 111 in his Bull *Filia Specialis* names Scotland a 'special daughter of the Holy See'.

18th century: last wolf killed

There is little evidence for what daily life was like in these early centuries. We can get a glimpse from the above notes and from a report by Pennant, written in 1769. At this time there were still no roads fit for horse and cart. Everything was carried in creels on someone's back – according to Pennant, this was woman's work and indeed this was still the case at the height of the herring fishing a century later. Oats and Bere were both grown, with hay for animal fodder. There were no barns, the crops being stacked in bee-hive shaped mounds, protected by thatching. (See the end page for a photo of a similar arrangement.)

Today's Travellers

Moving around by car or campervan does not preclude making close contact with the land! Here are two ideas for experiencing to some degree the lives of those early travellers.

Lochs and Rivers

Water has never been in short supply in Scotland and we tend to take it for granted. Today, we have a seemingly-limitless supply coming directly into our houses and have waterproof clothing to protect us from the source of this supply. The saints whose lives we are thinking about had a more complex relationship with the environment around them. One aspect that tends to be forgotten, which we have mentioned briefly already, is that the lochs and rivers were used as navigational aids, not just to be walked beside but to be travelled on. It would have been far easier to take a coracle up the river Thurso and across Loch More towards Achscoraclate than to walk there and even easier for the downward journey. Where walking was unavoidable, the lochs and rivers with which Caithness is so generously provided must have been useful for taking a refreshing bath at the end of a day's tramp. They must also have been an important source of fresh food for both the permanent resident and the traveller.

Today, we are not so dependent on the water-ways for transport but still use them for swimming and fishing. For the benefit of those of you who would like to share this experience with the saints of old, we include the following guides. Swimming in the rivers has not been covered – they can be fast-flowing and cold! It could also upset the fishermen.

Swimming

The following information is taken from 'Hills of the North Rejoice!' by Ralph MacGregor, available online from curlewcottage.com. I repeat my warning from the introduction that small, peaty lochans can be dangerous, as can the peat bogs surrounding them. Ralph MacGregor is a very experienced mountaineer, canoeist, cyclist and swimmer. Only try to emulate him if you are equally fit and experienced. Even then, do not do so alone!

This is a greatly edited list – we have removed lochs that are too distant from our routes or are unsuitable/dangerous for swimming. We have left some that are a good walk from our routes if they are particularly appealing and/or have a path to them. The numbers in brackets are grid references.

Loch Calder (070610) No shortage of places to swim.

Dunnet Head Lochs:- some fifteen, most very good for swimming, but Courtfall Loch 214740 and Northern Gate Loch 209719[45] are reedy pools not suitable for swimming or paddling. I have edited Ralph's list down to the following:

---

[45] The Northern Gate loch has recently been drained.

Loch of Bushta (195726) Good for swimming from South end where there is a nice sloping sandy bottom. Black Loch (near Red Geo) (185736) Surprisingly good loch for swimming, like a large swimming pool, went in from the north bank, peaty bottom but soon out of depth and fine for swimming. Nice location.

Grassy Loch (near road) (207743) Went in from South-East bank – a surprisingly good swim, stony/peaty bottom then deep, swam across to far shore which is a deep/floating bog suddenly ending in five-foot deep water. Could do widths!

Black Loch (near road, above Many Lochs) (203745) A good swimming pool, stony at South bank but shelves quite quickly into deep water, nice swim, some weed towards far shore.

Loch of Muirs (202734) A surprisingly good loch for safe swimming. From South-East bank, peaty/stony floor soon deep enough, could swim right across but still just touch bottom. Nice location

Loch Eilanach (070475) Nice swim to island.

Loch Gaineimh (050470) A very good loch for swimming with a sandy beach and sandy bottom.

Loch of Killimster (308560) A surprisingly good swim from the fishing jetty at the eastern end of the loch.

Loch Meadie (090480) Overlooked by the road so it is best to go in half way up the Western shore where a forestry track gives access. Good swimming.

Loch a Mhuilinn (Dorrery) (060568) Small but a good safe swimming pool, firm but soft bottom, about four feet deep.

Loch na Moine (938658) Good swimming, unusual clifftop location.

Loch More (080460) The classic swimming loch; you might even meet somebody else in the water off the sandy beaches along the Eastern shore.

Loch Rangag (178418) Shelves very steeply from the broch to deep water.

Loch Sarclet (343430) At the Southern end, you need to push through thick undergrowth to reach the bank. Once in, the stony bottom soon shelves to deep enough water for a good swim

Little Loch Scye (012554) Remarkably good for swimming – sandy shore, deep enough, not very stony, good setting

Loch Shurrery (045555) Best to swim from the Southern end of the loch on the Dorrery side where there is a small sandy beach and you are not overlooked

Loch Stemster (Achavanich) (190425) Stony.

The Trinkie (376495) Excellent salt-water outdoor swimming pool.

Loch Toftingall (190525) Now surrounded by plantations but still good for swimming from boat landing to West.

Loch Tuim Ghlais (978525) Perhaps the best loch of all.

Loch Watten (230560) The crannog at the Eastern end makes a nice objective (but was overgrown with nettles on my last visit!)

Loch of Yarrows (310440) Nice at Southern end where not overlooked.

Fishing[46]

Caithness has often been described as an angler's paradise, a county comprising somewhere in the region of 714 square miles of what can be best described as predominantly flat open moorland with big skies and breath-taking views. There are in the region of 100+ lochs in the county which, together with smaller lochans, rivers and streams of varying descriptions, provide a home for Atlantic salmon and sea trout returning to their natal rivers to spawn and resident brown trout, all wild indigenous fish. An almost impossible choice for an angler in deciding

---

[46] With thanks to Dave Martin for this section.

where to fish and what to fish for!

The start of the salmon fishing season varies from river to river usually in the months of January and February and ends in September or the first week in October. In the main, fly fishing is the permitted method for catching salmon although the skilled worm fisher can practice his/her art on one of the rivers in Caithness. Access to all rivers for salmon fishing is controlled and subject to local, and on some rivers, legally mandated catch and release policies which do vary between rivers. Advice on fishing for salmon in the county and the necessary permits can be obtained from a number of sources including Hugo Ross' tackle shop in Wick, Harpers emporium in Thurso and from websites run by the river fisheries and estate offices. These sources can, of course, also advise on fly and line choices and the currently productive parts of the rivers.

Sea Trout fishing is also available on one or two rivers and lochs in Caithness and details of this, together with season dates, tackle and flies can be obtained from the sources mentioned above.

The trout season starts on the 15th March each year and runs through until the 30th September although a small number of lochs in Caithness remain open until the 6th October. In the main, trout fishing is undertaken on the lochs but where the intention is to fish for trout on a river, advice should be sought from the relevant fishery or estate office to avoid conflict with fishery or estate staff and their associated activities. The 'right to roam' legislation provides for access over land and water but not necessarily to undertake any other activities on that land/water.[47]

Bank fishing is permitted on most of the lochs whilst a number also have boats which can be hired and details of these, together with associated permits, flies and directions can also be obtained from the Caithness tackle shops and the Dounreay Fly Fishing Association website (www.dffa.co.uk). One loch is an "any method" loch where spinning and bait fishing is also permitted. When considering fishing from a boat on any loch irrespective of size, it is essential to be aware of weather conditions and to wear a buoyancy aid, or preferably a lifejacket, at all times. If in doubt about the weather – don't go out. There is always another day!

If the plethora of loch and river fishing is not enough, there is always high-quality sea fishing to be had from either the Wick or Scrabster harbours. Depending on the time of year, cod, ling, haddock, mackerel and pollack can be found in good sizes and quantities. Shark fishing might also be available. Details for sea fishing trips can be obtained from either Hugo Ross in Wick or Harpers in Thurso.

---

47 Statutory Access Rights (Scottish Rights of Way and Access Society) The Land Reform (Scotland) Act 2003 (which came into force in 2005) gives everyone rights of access over land and inland water throughout Scotland, subject to specific exclusions set out in the Act and as long as they behave responsibly

The North Highlands

Having set the scene, we will now explore the sites of the Celtic saints who brought Christianity to Caithness or who were venerated in Caithness for other reasons. These sites have been linked to form six circular routes, four based in Thurso and two in Wick – the Northern Saints Trails. (See p. 139 for a map.) Only sites with specific names associated with them are included. As with the NPW, there are too many chapel sites, cairns and brochs to mention them all. For those interested, please see the HER map and other sources listed in the Bibliography.

Before we begin going round in circles, the numbering of the sites needs some explanation! These routes were designed with the North Coast 500 in mind.[48] So number 1 is Inverness and numbers 2-5 take the traveller up the west coast and along the north coast to Reay, which is number 6. The other coastal sites along to John O'Groats and down the east coast back to Inverness are numbered 7-34. Then the Caithness inland sites are numbered 35-50 in the order of the six routes.

Here are the notes on sites 1-5, taking the traveller from Inverness to the west coast and along the north coast to Strathnaver. Details of the east coast sites between Canisbay and Tain can be found in Part Two, although in the reverse order.

---

[48] The very popular circular tourist route for drivers starting in Inverness and taking the driver over to the west coast, along the north coast and down the east coast back to Inverness`.

Sites 35-50 make up the circular routes within Caithness. This information, with photographs for most of the sites, can also be found on the Northern Saints Trails page of the NPW website at www.northernpilgrimsway.co.uk.

1. Inverness   Local Saints: Columba; John; Adamnan; Kenneth; Kessog; Ernan
Inverness is known as the capital of the Highlands and Inverness Castle makes a dramatic starting point for any tour of the north.

St Erchard (or Irchard/Yrchard/Merchard) could also be listed as belonging to Inverness as his strongest links are with the Great Glen, especially the Glenmoriston area. Some sources also link him with Strathglass, not too far from Brora, and with Caithness.

2. Beauly Priory   Local saint: Tarlogan
The name (*beau lieu* or 'beautiful place') was given to the area by the French monks who founded the abbey in about 1230. They belonged to the Valliscaulian order, as did the monks of Pluscarden Abbey, founded at about the same time. After the Reformation, the building was left to become a ruin and the land was given to the Episcopal bishop of Ross.

3. Applecross   Local Saints: Maelrubha
From Beauly to Lochcarron, there is no information on specific local saints. From there onwards through

Applecross, north to Durness and along the north coast to Farr, the only name is that of Maelrubha.

4. Balnakiell   Local Saint: Maelrubha

5. Strathnaver   Local   Saints: Maelrubha, Donan, Martin, Cormack, Diman
The village of Farr lies at the mouth of Strathnaver and hosts the Strathnaver Museum, where much can be learnt about the history of this area. There is also a copy of the magnificent Farr Stone. There is a Strathnaver Trail following the river inland and showing the site where Maelrubha is thought to be buried. Cormack's connection to this area rests on a rather vague claim that he settled on Colm Island (Eilean nan Naomh – The Saint's Island). He has stronger connections with Orkney. Diman also has links with Orkney (the island of Daimsey) but dies in Strathnaver in 670.

28. Tain itself – see Part Two. The area south of Tain is associated with Comgan and Kiltearn parish church on the outskirts of Alness is named after him.
Continue on the A9 to the roundabout just before the Cromarty Bridge, take the second exit onto the A862 and continue to Dingwall.

29. Dingwall   Local Saint: Clement
The Gaelic name means 'place of cabbages' which may be a link with the nearby Beauly Abbey whose founding order, the Valliscaulians, came from Val-des-Choux (Valley of the Cabbages) near Dijon,

France. The current name derives from the Norse 'Thing', a meeting place. The landing place for trading boats from Scandinavia was near the church, a logical place for such a meeting point. (In Shetland, the place called Tingwall is close to the church.) The church dedication to Clement also suggests Viking links – see the entry on Clement in the Alphabetical List of Saints.

From Dingwall, either continue on the A862 through Beauly and back to Inverness or return to the A9 and continue to Inverness via the Cromarty Bridge, the Black Isle and the Kessock Bridge.

Some Off-Route Sites

30. Portmahomack   Local Saint: <u>Colman</u>
There have been extensive excavations here, uncovering evidence of a large monastic settlement dating from the 8th century. The old parish church is now a museum tracing the history of the area and the excavations and displaying the various finds.

31. The Cloutie Well   Local Saint: <u>Curitan</u>
Tradition says that, if one leaves a piece of clothing from the affected part of the body, healing will occur. If anyone removes a piece of clothing from the site, they will develop the illness of the original owner.

  The post-Reformation authorities tried to ban these practices, regarding them as idolatrous. However sites such as this one that were associated with healing tended to survive. Indeed, they were more important to ordinary people than the cathedrals.

To get there, turn left (assuming that you are travelling south!) at the Tore roundabout onto the A832 towards the village of Munlochy. The well is on the right-hand side, surrounded by trees.

32. Rosemarkie   Local Saint: Moluag

As the system of church governance became more organised, Rosemarkie was the main centre for the north until the area was divided into the three dioceses of Caithness, Ross and Moray. St Curitan/Boniface built the first Scottish stone church in the 'Roman Style' here in the 8th century.

The Groam House Museum is best known for its collection of carved stones.

33. Fortrose   Local Saint: Curitan/Boniface

Impressive remains of the cathedral still exist.

34 The Kessock Bridge   Local Saint: Kessog

Before the modern bridge, there was a small ferry linking North and South Kessock. Originally, it was used by pilgrims on their way to Tain.

Having explored the NC500, we can now take a look at the smaller circles that make up the Northern Saints Trails. On the next page is a copy of the inner fold of a NST leaflet showing the six routes. It is followed by a description of the routes.

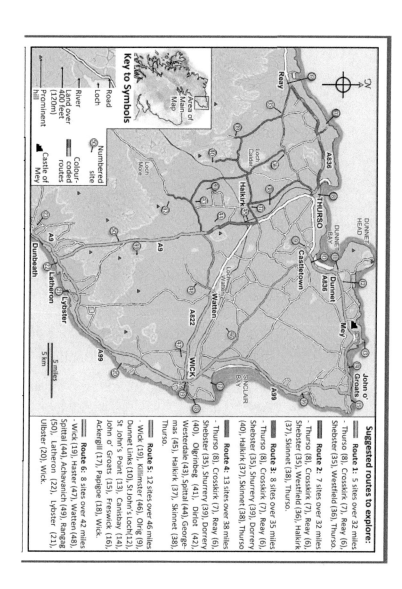

Suggested routes to explore:

Route 1: 5 sites over 32 miles
- Thurso (8), Crosskirk (7), Reay (6), Shebster (35), Westfield (36), Thurso.

Route 2: 7 sites over 32 miles
- Thurso (8), Crosskirk (7), Reay (6), Shebster (35), Westfield (36), Halkirk (37), Skinnet (38), Thurso.

Route 3: 8 sites over 35 miles
- Thurso (8), Crosskirk (7), Reay (6), Shebster (35), Shurrery (39), Dorrery (40), Halkirk (37), Skinnet (38), Thurso.

Route 4: 13 sites over 38 miles
- Thurso (8), Crosskirk (7), Reay (6), Shebster (35), Shurrery (39), Dorrery (40), Olgrinbeg (41), Dirlot (42), Westerdale (43), Spittal (44), Georgemas (45), Halkirk (37), Skinnet (38), Thurso.

Route 5: 12 sites over 46 miles
- Wick (19), Killimster (46), Olrig (9), Dunnet Links (10), St John's Loch (12), St John's Point (13), Canisbay (14), John o' Groats (15), Freswick (16), Ackergill (17), Papigoe (18), Wick.

Route 6: 8 sites over 42 miles
- Wick (19), Haster (47), Watten (48), Spittal (44), Achavanich (49), Rangag (50), Latheron (22), Lybster (21), Ulbster (20), Wick.

Routes 1-4 (Thurso)

8. Thurso (Thor's river)   Local Saint: <u>Peter</u>.
Dedications to Peter began with <u>Curitan</u>/Boniface (see
the Alphabetical List of Saints).

If you are driving, there are two possible car parks.
Shore Street car park is a few minutes walk from the
start of the route and from Old St Peter's Kirk. If you
have a campervan, you might prefer to use the larger
park on the riverside.

   Start at the North Coast Visitor Centre, where
there is a display of carved stones and other artefacts
from early times. These include the Ulbster Stone, the
Skinnet Stone, the Watenan stone, baptismal fonts
from St. Thomas' at Skinnet and Old St Peters Kirk,
Thurso, a cross slab from Canisbay and two memorial
stones from Old St Peter's Kirk.

   Then follow Shore Street towards the river and
admire the ruined St Peter's church. The apsidal cell
is typical of the 12th century, the nave and transept
belong to the 16th or 17th century. In the West wall,
there is a gravestone dated to the middle of the 14th
century. It may have been founded by Gilbert, bishop
of Caithness, about 1220. It was used as a parish
church until 1832 and, early in the 18th century, was
used as a court-house and prison.

   A path, Victoria Walk, follows the shore-line
from the harbour at the mouth of Thurso River
towards Scrabster. The original bishop's palace was
built at the mouth of the Wolf Burn along Victoria
Walk. Any remains have been washed out to sea. It

had probably been built when Caithness was overseen by the bishop of Orkney, who owned lands in Caithness and continued to receive tithes from Dunnet and Canisbay for some time after the separate diocese of Caithness was created (c.1150).[49] Looking back towards the town, the modern houses are on Pennyland estate, possibly so called because of the penny tax paid by householders to the bishop or because 'ounceland' and 'pennyland' were used for the assessment of land values over many centuries.[50])

Take the A836 from Thurso towards Reay. Approximately five miles along this road and just before the wooded dip that is the Forss burn and bridge, turn right and continue for 2 miles to the car park.

7. Crosskirk (suggests a dedication to the Holy Cross or Rood)   Local saints: Mary; Peter

This is among the oldest still-visible church buildings in Caithness, dating from the 12th century. It is known as St Mary's Chapel. However some records give the dedication as to St Peter. There is a spring nearby known as St Mary's well and a graveyard where gravestones can still be seen. The doorway is unusually low and there are two theories about this – it means that everyone entering this holy space has to bow to the altar and/or it prevents enemies from rushing in and overpowering the congregation.

---

49 See Crawford p.149
50 See the journal of the Scottish Society of Northern Studies, vol 24 pp 69-70

Just 30 yards from the chapel, near the sea, was the remains of a large Iron Age broch.[51] A story that a symbol stone from the broch was given to the king of Denmark by Sir George Sinclair is not quite accurate. The stone came from Shebster and was given to the Danish archaeologist who found it. On his instructions, it was sent to the museum in Denmark, where it was lost. The broch itself was investigated and then bulldozed into the sea (see Caithness Field Club Bulletin 1985, available on the Caithness.org website).

Crosskirk would be a natural landing spot for pilgrims from Orkney when weather and tide meant navigating round the western side of Hoy. It could also have been an overnight stopping point for pilgrims from further west. Crosskirk is in line with Shebster, where there was a chapel site dedicated to St Magnus. From here the pilgrim would follow what is now known as the Ca na Catanach over to the Strath of Kildonan.

From Crosskirk, return to the A836 and turn right towards Reay. Care is needed when approaching the A836 as there is no 'give way' sign on the minor road, which continues in a straight line on the other side of the A836, and the driver could easily not realise that he/she is approaching a junction where other drivers have priority. Continue on the A836 for 5.5 miles.

---

[51] The earliest known tower broch was found at Crosskirk. I have not been able to check whether it is this one that was demolished or another one.

6. Reay   Local Saint: <u>Colman</u>.

Note the market cross in the centre of the village.

The current church, to the north of the road, is similar in style to those in Dunnet and Canisbay. They all date from the 15th or 16th century and are on or near the sites of older churches. In Reay, the older church is on the south side of the road opposite the school.

Remains of the original church can be seen in the NE corner of the old graveyard, which also contains several tombstones with heraldic shields. The carved stone known as Reay 1, which was found over an 18thcentury grave, is set into the West wall of these remains. It is decorated with a fine cross. There are two Pictish stones at Sandside House, Reay. As this is a private house, the public cannot see them.

Information about them can be found at http://portal.historicenvironment.scot/designation/SM616 and https://canmore.org.uk/site/318979/creagan-a-bheannaich-chapel-and-graveyard.

Various local names indicate that the area was a significant religious centre, for example *Lochan a' Chleirich* (the loch of the clergyman), *Cnoc-an-Eireannaich* (the Irishman's Hill, probably Donnan).

Turn back along the A836 and turn right just after the Isauld Bridge on the road to Shebster. (There may have been a chapel among the sand dunes to the NE of the Isauld burn, 300-400 yards from its mouth.)

35. Shebster   Local Saint: <u>Magnus</u>

There was a chapel here (map reference MHG997) dedicated to Magnus, suggesting that this site was on a pilgrimage route to/from St Magnus Cathedral,

Kirkwall, probably for travellers crossing the Pentland Firth via Crosskirk.

At Shebster, the traveller has two options – Routes 1 and 2 or the longer routes 3 and 4. For route1 and route 2, continue Eastwards for just over three miles to Westfield, which is 6 miles from Reay.

36. Westfield   Local Saint: <u>Drostan</u>
Not far from the road on the east of the village and in a field behind farm buildings is a graveyard which was in use until recently. There is a sign 'St Trostan's Cemetery 600m, Achnavast 1.8Km'. It is accessed via a track that turns off the road to the right through the farm steading and along to a parking/turning point. Leave the car here and walk along the fenced-off path through the field to the gravesite. Built into the SE wall is an oval block of sandstone, presumed to be the font of the chapel dedicated to St Drostan that once stood here

Route 1 now returns to Thurso, via Glengolly. It is 6 miles from Westfield to the riverside car park in Thurso. Route 2 back-tracks to the left-hand turning for Halkirk via Calder. About 1 ½ miles down this road, there is a bench on the verge and a small parking place. Here one can sit to admire the view or take the path down to the lochside.

37. Halkirk (In the Orkneyinga Saga, this is Ha Kirkia/Kirkja – the High Kirk) Local Saints: Fergus, Gilbert, Tarlogan, Katherine (with sites dedicated to Ciaran, Peter and Colum nearby).

On the edge of Halkirk, a road branches to the right towards the river at Gerston, where there was a chapel dedicated to St Katherine. There is nothing left to see. Continue to the main road and turn right into the village. Turn left into Sinclair Street and drive along to the site of the old church. When the bishopric of Orkney separated from that of the mainland, the Caithness bishop moved his residence from Scrabster to Halkirk. His palace was on the opposite side of the river from the present Braal castle, near the current ruined church building, where an ancient chapel existed. It was made famous by the burning of Bishop Adam, in 1222. It is possible that the chapel was the private place of worship of the bishop and his household but the main bishop's cathedral was on the Thurso side of the village at Skinnet. Braal castle marks the site of a ford across the River Thurso, presumably providing a walking route from the bishop's palace to the cathedral at Skinnet.

Return to the main road and turn right towards Thurso.

38. Skinnet   Local Saint: Thomas

Skinnet Farm is just outside Halkirk on the right-hand side of the road as you go towards Thurso. The site of the cathedral lies between the modern farmhouse and the River Thurso. The claim of this site to be the cathedral rests partly on the quality of the sculpted stone found at this site and now kept in the North Coast Visitor Centre. Other clues are the number of dedications in the area and the remains of earlier buildings, one of which may have been an abbey, as the Gaelic place-name is *An Abaid.*

Route 2 now returns to Thurso. Routes 3 and 4 follow routes 1 and 2 to Shebster. Then they turn right towards Broubster and Shurrery.

39. Shurrery   House of Blessings (not Benedict!)
The site is sometimes assumed to have the dedication 'Benedict' but this is a mis-translation of the Latin '*Benediction*' and the Gaelic '*Bheannaich*', both meaning 'blessing'. The croft land (HER map reference MHG18167) is known as *Tigh a' Bheannaich* (House of Blessing) and is said to be the site of a chapel, well and burial ground (HER map references MHG39490 and MHG39489). This title suggests a rest-house for travellers, hence the suggestion that a pilgrimage route existed through Shurrery. Beaton tells us that

> 'The chapel, as the Rev John Kerr, Shurrery, informs me, stood close to the river. Two corner stones are still visible. There was a burial ground here also; the last burial in it took place about eighty years ago. About 150 yards to the south is *Tobar a'mhannaich*, the monks well. To the Westward stand the ruins of the Priests House (*Tigh a' Mhannaich*) which was occupied as late as some fifty years ago.'[52]

---

[52] Ecc Hist p.333

40. Dorrery   Local Saint: Gavin (see
the alphabetical list for an explanation of the name).

From Shurrery, follow the road Eastwards to meet the
B870. Apr. half way along this road, past Brawlbin
Farm, there is a road turning right towards Dorrery.
This road ends after two miles, with the entrance to
Dorrery Lodge ahead. There is a small parking area to
the left. A track to the left leads towards fields. At the
second gate the traveller can see a walled-in graveyard
in the distance. Within this graveyard are the ruins of
Gavin's kirk or Temple Gavin. The surrounding land
once belonged to the bishops of Caithness. (Please do
not go through these fields if there is livestock in them
or if doing so might damage crops or otherwise upset
the owner.) To the right of the entrance to the Lodge
is a path signposted 'Ben Dorrery Hill'. At the corner
of the Lodge garden and just before the farm
buildings, this path branches, with the right branch
going up the hill and the left meandering inland
towards Loch Caluim – part of the Ca na Catanach
droving road. It is worth going along this path until
you are clear of the buildings as you then get an
attractive view of the graveyard and surrounding
fields. On a good day, it is also worth following the
path up to the top of Ben Dorrery Hill, where there is
a panoramic view of Caithness.

Just past the junction with the B870, Routes 3
and 4 separate. Route 3 continues on to Halkirk and
joins Route 2. Route 4 branches off to the right and
continues on the B870 for 1 mile to Olgrinbeg.

41. Olgrinbeg   Local Saint: Peter

Access to this site is through Olgrinbeg farm. There are the remains of a chapel dedicated to Peter on the bank of the Olgrinbeg Burn about ½ mile above its junction with the Thurso River. The field beside the chapel is called An Abair and a nearby hill is Appat Hill. Some sources suggest that this indicates an earlier dedication to a Celtic saint, others that it suggests that the land was owned by the abbot/bishop. Perhaps this is one of the dedications influenced by Curitan/Boniface.

42: Dirlot   Local Saint: Colum/Columba

This site is in a field used by the farmer to graze animals and care must be taken not to disturb them.

From Olgrinbeg, travel towards Westerdale for a few miles. Where the B870 takes a sharp turn left towards Mybster, there is a minor road branching off to the right. This leads to Loch More. About two miles along this road an even smaller road branches off to the left towards Dirlot. There is a 'Private' sign at the junction but it refers to the fishing rights on the river, not to the road. At the farm buildings a gate to the right leads into a field and the path goes to the walled-in graveyard. Within the graveyard was a chapel dedicated to Colum although no trace of it can be seen now. Some maps and sources give the dedication here as 'Columba' but see the entry for 'Colum' in the Alphabetical List of Saints for my reasons for disputing this. There was a holy well north of the graveyard near the shepherd's house called *Tobar Chalum-Cille*. An attractive view of the river passing through a gorge can be seen from the path just past the graveyard.

An optional extra: Return to the minor road, turn left towards Loch More and continue for about three miles, passing Strathmore Lodge. Keep to the left until close to the loch, where there is space to park the car. The track continues for over two miles to Achscoraclate, where the remains of a cottage can be seen, but is too rough to take a car. Achscoraclate was the site of a chapel and holy well dedicated to St Bridget and was probably on a pilgrimage route through the county.

43. Westerdale   Local Saint: Drostan
St Trostan's Chapel and graveyard can no longer be seen. They lie under vegetation ½ mile north of Westerdale, near the Westerdale Mill but on the opposite bank of the river.

Continue on the B870 until it meets the A9 at Mybster. Turn left and you are almost at the village of Spittal.

44. Spittal (hospital or hostel for travellers)   Local Saint: Magnus
The dedication to Magnus indicates that this was on a pilgrimage route to and from St Magnus Cathedral on Orkney (but see the entry about Spittal in Part Two). The site consisted of a hospital/hostel, chapel and graveyard, the remains of which are 250 yards NW of Spittal Mains farm. They can just be seen from the main road but there is no safe stopping place. If you want to visit the site, turn left towards Spittal Mains,

where there is a small parking space. You can then walk to the site. Please be aware that this is a working farm and you are walking through the farm steading.

The graveyard was the traditional resting place of the Clan Gunn. The earliest known reference to the hospital is a charter dated 1476 granted by King James III to William Sinclair, son of William, Earl of Caithness.

From Spittal, continue on the A9. At Georgemas Junction, you can stop at the station.

45 Georgemas   Local Saints: George; Mary; Katherine

The station is so called as it is near the hill where the St George's Day Fair was held. It is also near the Sibster Burn, associated with chapels dedicated to Mary and Katherine. The sources are rather confusing here, as they place the Marykirk ½ mile S of Sibster House near Wick River, which is not in this area. They may also be confusing St Katherine's chapel with that at Gerston, on the other side of Halkirk.

George is not a local name. Perhaps the dedication came from someone returning from the Crusades, which do have a connection with St George (see the entry for Spittal in Part Two and for St George in Part Four for more information).

On leaving Georgemas, follow the A9 to the turn–off for Halkirk and join routes 2 and 3. If you are in a hurry, you can stay on the A9 into Thurso and the end of the trail.

Routes 5 and 6 (Wick)

Route 5 (the north loop)

19. Wick (from the Norse 'Vic', a bay).
Local saints: Fergus (6th or 8th century): Ninian(6th century); Francis (?13th century)

The north loop starts at the Parish Church, dedicated to St Fergus, on the main road at the northern end of the town. For details, go to the entry on Wick in Part Two.

46. Killimster   Local saint: Duthac
From St Fergus church, take the Thurso road – the B876 – for five miles to Killimster. Pull into the lay-by on the left just at the top of a rise (there is a group of modern houses to the right). You are now looking over Killimster Moss to the south, sometimes known as the Kirk Moss, where St Duthac's chapel (or Dudoch's as it was known locally) was. The chapel was built on some raised ground about a mile West of Loch Killimster and near the Burn of Kirk Stains. It is now surrounded by very boggy ground and is not readily accessible.

9. Olrig   Local saints: Drostan; Colum
Having admired the view and wondered at the dedication of those early saints who lived and worked here so long ago, continue towards Castletown. On the edge of the village, turn left with the primary school on your right and drive apr ½ mile on a single-track

151

road. Take the first turn right and continue a short distance to Olrig graveyard on the left. Just past the road taking you to the entrance of the old graveyard is a parking space for the new graveyard. You can park here and walk through the new graveyard to access the old one. In this graveyard was a chapel dedicated to Drostan/Trothan. This was built in 1663 to replace the chapel near the shore on the Dunnet Links, dedicated to St Coomb (or Colum or Colm – see next entry). This is still referred to by locals as Coombs Kirk. The replacement was used as the parish church until 1840. A socketed plinth of an ancient churchyard cross is on the south side of the building beside the Selkie's grave (see the entry for Drostan in the Alphabetical List of Saints for details). This grave has a concrete border identifying it. It is reputed to never dry out. Another legend is that Drostan, or Trothan as he is known at this site, is buried on the same site, which would explain the cross.

This graveyard can be treacherous in damp weather as much of the ground is covered in graveslabs which themselves are covered in moss, making them slippery to walk on.

Traces of a building which may have been a monastery and/or nunnery have been found in the field to the east of the graveyard.

10. Dunnet Links   Local saints: Colum; Colm
Return to the main road, turn left and follow the curve round to the junction with the Thurso-John o' Groats road – the A836. Turn right and continue past the garden centre on the right. Ahead is Dunnet Bay.

There is a small parking area just off the road to the left where you can get a view of the sweep of the bay. If you are walking along the beach, be aware that, depending on the tides and the amount of rainfall, there is an area of sinking sands not far from the car park. It is safer to keep to the stones and grass until the first burn.

As you drive along the edge of the bay, known as the Dunnet Links, you will notice sand dunes on either side of the road. Some of these are just that – sand, but some contain ancient settlements. There is also a post-Reformation manse that was completely covered by sand during a storm and a chapel site dedicated to Colum/Coomb – the Coombs Kirk mentioned above. Local legend is that the minister had to climb out of a skylight in the roof, so sudden and violent was the sandstorm.

Towards the east end of the bay and on the right is Dunnet Forest. If you have a dog in the car, this is an excellent place to give it some exercise, especially if the weather does not lend itself to a walk on the beach. Just past the forest entry and on the left is Dunnet Caravan Park and the Seadrift Centre. The Centre is run by the Highland Council Ranger Service and contains displays on local geology, flora and fauna. It is only open in the Summer.

11. Dunnet and area   Local saints: John; Mary
Continue past the caravan site to Dunnet village. Just before the hotel and behind its car park is Dunnet Church of Scotland parish church. This building dates back to the 15th century and is similar to the churches

at Reay and Canisbay. While one source says that it was dedicated to Anne, it seems more likely that the dedication was to Mary as the local fair is still known as the Marymas Fair and until recently was held on the first Saturday after the Feast of the Assumption of Our Lady on 15th August. It is now held on the last Saturday of August to ensure that it does not clash with the school holidays.

Dedications to Mary and the apostles suggest a post-Celtic beginning or a re-dedication. We have seen that the area to the west of Dunnet is linked with Drostan, Colum and Colm, so perhaps they could also lay some claim to the village itself.

12. St John's Loch   Local saint: John the Baptist
Just past the village lies St John's Loch. Local tradition says that it is so called after John the Baptist because its waters were used for baptisms. It is one of several local places that were thought to have healing powers and there was a tradition of walking round the edge of the loch three times on Midsummer morning and praying for a cure. The edge of the loch is still a right of way but is used today by fishermen rather than penitents (to fish, you need a permit, obtainable at the hotel or fishing tackle shop on the edge of the village). Access can be gained via either the new harbour on the north shore, off Hunspow Road (B855), or the old harbour on the south side, off Corsback Road (A836). There was a chapel at the south-east end of the loch, now only a slightly raised area. It can be accessed by following the edge of the loch in an Easterly direction from the old harbour. The loch drains by a small burn

that runs close to the church and into the bay. Traces of an early settlement have been found near the mouth of the burn.

In order to include Dunnet Head in your travels, you need to turn left just past the hotel and distillery and follow the B855 round the sharp bend and along to Brough with St John's Loch on your right. At Brough, turn left and continue to the end of the single-track road.

On the west side of Dunnet Head is an inlet known as Chapel Geo. Here a hermit built himself a shelter and chapel. If you are interested in visiting this site, you will need stout walking boots and preferably a map. As you will be walking along the edge of a cliff, this is only suitable for pets on leads and children who can be relied on to stay on the path. Do not attempt the walk in poor visibility or a strong wind. Having said that, it can be a lovely walk! Take the B855 from the village but, instead of going round the curve, go straight ahead following the sign for Mary Anne's cottage. At the T junction either:

a) turn up the hill and park the car at the end of the road (there is room for apr. three cars to park). Go through the wooden gate and follow the path to almost the top of the cliff and, instead of going down to the Peedie Sands, take the path (more of a sheep track than a proper path!) to the right. Go past the stone building (a comparatively modern structure), up the hill and along the cliff edge until you come to a cutting in the cliff face where you can look down onto a stony shore – Chapel Geo. Allow about an hour for the return journey.

b) if you are interested in the North Highland Way, you might prefer to turn left at the T junction and go down to Dwarwick pier, where there is ample parking. You can then follow the North Highland Way path over the hill and towards Peedie Sands. At the sands, instead of going down to the shore, turn up the hill and turn left onto the path described above.

Return to Brough and continue along the coast through Ham, Scarfskerry, Harrow and Mey. On the left at Ham are the ruins of chambered cairns, called souterrains on some maps. These have a unique structure and their description is reminiscent of Tolkein's hobbit houses. Once past Harrow, you will see the Castle of Mey on the right. Now open to the public in the Summer, this was for many years the holiday home of the Queen Mother. It originally belonged to the Sinclair family who also owned the estates around Rosslyn Chapel in Mid- Lothian and there are various legends linking the two buildings.

13. St John's Point   Local Saint: John

Once past the castle, the promontory ahead is St John's Point and the remains of a chapel and wall can be seen. Access is possible by parking at the corner (one car at a time only) where the road takes a sharp turn south and walking back through the field. The usual warnings about fencing and livestock apply.

14. Canisbay   Local saint: Drostan

From St John's point the road joins the A836 and passes through Gills to Canisbay. The third of the county's pre-Reformation churches stands at the side of the road. The building is usually open to the public during the summer. It is built on the site of an ancient chapel dedicated to Drostan, and there are records of it going back to 1222. Drostan belonged to the 6th century and is the most-named saint in Caithness, suggesting that Canisbay was an important centre.

15. John O'Groats   Local Saint: Mary
From Canisbay, continue through Huna to the T junction. Turn left to John O'Groats. This was thought for many years to be the most northerly point on the British mainland but more modern measuring techniques have re-allocated this honour to Dunnet Head. However it is still the end of the road – or the beginning, depending on your direction of travel. So do spend some time here before moving to the site of St Mary's chapel. This is on the 'John O'Groats Way', which is signposted. The chapel was sited at the far end of the beach. If you want to look for the rare cowrie shells (known locally as Groaty Buckies), you need to go on to the next beach!

On a clear day, it is worth continuing your walk up the hill towards the lighthouse. Then follow the cliff edge (but not too close!) for a spectacular view of the Stacks of Duncansby. A short distance along is a geo whose cliff faces teem with bird life.

16. Freswick   Local Saint: Modan
On returning to the main road, take the A99 south to Freswick with its sweeping bay. The first left turn after the one to Skirsa is a private road to Freswick Castle. Here there is a comparatively modern (about

350 years old) chapel and mausoleum built on the site of an ancient chapel dedicated to St Modan. The mausoleum is easily identified by its round windows. The original chapel was much venerated and local people continued to practice 'popish rites' here long after the Reformation (see 'Lest we Forget' p. 101 and others.)

17. Ackergill   Local Saint: Drostan
From Freswick, continue on the A99 to the junction with the Thurso-Wick road. To the left just before the junction is Ackergill bay, where there was a chapel dedicated to Drostan. There is easy access to the site but nothing remains other than a small cairn erected by the Clan Gunn Society in memory of those killed in a clan battle (see under 'Ackergill' in the section 'Following Braid Three' for details). At the junction, turn left towards Wick. Turn left into Henrietta Street and follow the road signs for Papigoe. They will take you right onto Girnigoe Street and then left onto Willowbank, which takes you out of the town and towards Staxigoe and Papigoe.

18. Papigoe   Local Saint: Ninian
St Ninian's chapel was situated on the cliff edge but nothing remains, although there are still local people who know of its existence. Some researchers believe that this chapel was actually situated closer to the centre of town at the lower bridge or where the lighthouse now is, but the name 'Papigoe' suggests church-owned land and is a more probable site. The dedication to Ninian does not necessarily mean that

Ninian himself visited Wick although some researchers argue that he could have done so while returning from a mission to Orkney and Shetland. Others point out that the prefix 'papi' is associated with the Northumbrian wander-cult of St Ninian and that it is far more likely that some of this group found their way up the coast to Wick and dedicated a chapel to their patron. 'Papi' comes from the early Irish 'pupu', 'popa' ('father', 'priest') and became 'papar' in Norse, where it was used for the hermits and wandering monks to be found around the coast of Scotland. So the Vikings, on finding a community of monks, called the harbour 'papi-Gjo' or 'the inlet of the papas'.

Return along Willowbank and take the Scalesburn road to the left down to the lower bridge, take right at the mini roundabout and again at the next mini-roundabout, follow the road across the bridge, through the traffic lights and round the corner to take you back to St Fergus Church, your starting point.

Route 6 (the south loop)

19. Wick   Local Saints: Fergus; Ninian
The start point for this route is the same as for the northern loop – St Fergus church. This time, head towards the town centre. At the mini roundabout, turn 2nd left up the hill and past the hospital on your right. At the traffic lights, turn right towards Thurso on the A882 and drive two miles to the village of Haster.

47. Haster   Local Saint: Cuthbert
St Cuthbert came from the borders and is best known as the Prior and Abbot of Lindisfarne. The site dedicated to him lies 200 yards ESE of Upper Haster farm house at the lower end of a cultivated field on the Burn of Haster and about 100 yards W of the Achairn burn. There is no obvious means of access.

48. Watten   Local Saints: Katherine; Fumac; Magnus; Tarlogan
From Haster, continue on the A882 to Watten. For more information on Watten, see Part Two.

On entering the village, take the right turn onto the B870. At the sharp corner, a narrow road goes off to the left to the site of the chapel at The Clow on the banks of the Scouthal Burn. This road is narrow and twisty, with deep ditches on either side and barbed wire on fences but without a proper turning place. So, while the remains of the chapel are still visible near the farmhouse, the site is perhaps best visited on foot, if at all. The following directions are currently awaiting further exploration.
     Continuing a short distance on the B870, the area of Wester-Watten is on the right at the edge of Loch Watten but Wester-Watten Moss is further south, to the right at the end of the track going past Scouthal and The Clow. One of these sites was where a fair used to be held around the time of the feast-day of St Magnus on 16th April, known in the Middle Ages as Magnusmas. This suggests that it was on a pilgrimage route to and from St Magnus Cathedral on

Orkney. Assuming that the pilgrims were meaning to pass through Spittal, they could have passed through either site as there are chapels at The Clow and at Dunn, along the loch-side from Wester-Watten. We are following the B870, which by-passes both of these areas. As it moves inland away from the village, it takes sharp left and right turns. The second road on the right after these turns leads to Markethall and the area of Dunn.

49. Ballachly by Achavanich   Local   Saint: Triduana

Continue on the B870 until it joins the A9 at Mybster, just south of Spittal. Turn left and follow the A9 to Achavanich, which is clearly signposted. Take the single-track road to the left and park at the shore of Loch Stemster. Admire the standing stones, then turn and take the track along the west side of the loch, branch left again and continue to the ruined graveyard at Ballachly. Here is the site of the 'resting place' of St Triduana where Bishop John was cured of blindness. St Triduana has a shrine at Restalrig in Edinburgh which is her most likely burial site, so the site at Ballachly is not her grave but may have had a relic of her buried there. The graveyard is apr four miles from the car park and is for walkers only.

50. Rangag   Local Saint: Ciaran

Continuing a short distance on the A9 southwards you will see Loch Rangag on your right. There are the remains of a building clearly visible on a spit of land not far from the road. Some sources refer to this as a broch, others as Greystell Castle. The literature of the Caithness Broch Project calls it a castle, so that is the most likely description.

This area is associated with St Ciaran, who is also linked with Latheron, and the inland areas around the heads of the Thurso and Rumsdale rivers.

22. Latheron   Local Saint: Curitan; Ciaran
There was a chapel between the road and the sea, where the road curves towards the sea on its way to Latheron. The site can be accessed by following the sign to the Old Church in the village, which is now the Clan Gunn Heritage Centre.

At this point, the route goes north but the traveller might want to take a diversion south a few miles to Dunbeath where there is a heritage museum, tea room and toilets. A short distance up the Dunbeath River is the House of Peace, site number 23. The Laidhay Croft Museum is just north of Dunbeath.

21. Lybster   Local Saint: Mary
There was a chapel dedicated to Mary on the road down to the harbour. No remains of the chapel exist. However the Waterlines Visitor Centre at the harbour is well worth a visit. For further details, go to 'Lybster' in Part Two.

20 Ulbster   Local Saint: Martin
The Ulbster stone is now kept in the North Coast Visitor Centre, Thurso and there are no remains locally. The old Thrumster Railway Station is now a museum.

19. Wick   Local Saints: Fergus, Ninian
As you approach the centre of the town, you will pass the hospital on your left. At the bottom of the hill is a mini-roundabout. Go ahead onto Bridge Street and follow the road through the town to your starting point at St Fergus Church.

Optional extra – turn right at the mini-roundabout, park wherever is suitable and walk to the gable end of the MacKay's Hotel, which is on Ebenezer Street, the shortest street in the world.

Another optional extra (again, this has not been tested recently, so check the route on a map before setting off) – cross the bridge, take the first turn to the left after the traffic lights and park at the car park on the riverside. On the hill behind the hotel is St Fergus church, your starting point. If you have the time, and the weather is reasonable, you can walk up the north bank of the Wick River to the point where the Achairn Burn (which passes under the bridge at Haster) joins the Wick River. There is a 'Mary ford' (no longer usable!) at this point of the river. Just above the river bank is the remains of St Mary's chapel. For long after the Reformation, people would visit this chapel on the first Sunday after the new moon. The Wick kirk session records of 1732 say that people still visited St Mary's Chapel on the first Sunday after a new moon, where they would bow and kneel in prayer. The baptismal font from the Sibster chapel is at Stirkoke House

Post Codes for the Sites

Many of our sites are not readily visible from the road or no longer have any physical remains. However there are records of their existence and the sites can be identified with the help of maps. The most detailed and accurate map for our purposes is that compiled by the Highland Council Archaeology Department, to be found at www.her.highland.gov. Ordinance Survey maps also mark many of the sites that I mention. Post codes are the least accurate guides. However they can be useful to reassure the traveller that they are in the correct general area. The post codes may refer to a nearby building rather than the actual site. When used with on-line route planners, they give fairly accurate locations. (For example, www.rac.co.uk/route-planner/ or www.google.co.uk/maps/.)

Arranged by route

	Place	Post code
8	Thurso	KW14 8AJ North Coast Visitor Centre
7	Crosskirk	KW14 7XY Forss House Hotel
6	Reay	KW14 7RG Bridgend House
34	Shebster	KW14 7QZ the garage
35	Westfield	KW14 7QN Bridge of Westfield
36	Gerston	KW14 6XQ houses
37	Halkirk	KW12 6XY Ulbster Arms Hotel
38	Skinnet	KW12 6XF the farm
39	Shurrery	KW14 7RB Shurrery Kirk

40	Dorrery	KW12 6YW the lodge
41	Olgrinbeg	KW12 6XJ the farm
42	Dirlot	KW12 6UP Dirlot Cottage
43	Westerdale	KW12 6UP old church
44	Spittal	KW1 5XR the quarry
45	Georgemas	KW12 6XA station house
19	Wick	KW1 4BS St Fergus Church
46	Killimster	KW1 4RX Killimster farm
9	Olrig	KW14 8UA C'town primary school
10	Dunnet Links	KW14 8TX garden centre
11	Dunnet Church	KW14 8XD Marymas Cottages
12	St John's Loch, Dunnet	KW14 8XQ Old Schoolhouse
13	St John's Point	KW14 8XL
14	Canisbay	KW1 4YB Kirkstyle
15	John O'Groats	KW1 4YR tourist info point
16	Freswick	KW1 4XX castle
17	Ackergill	KW1 4RG farm
18	Papigoe	KW1 5SZ farm
47	Haster	KW1 5SZ farm
48	Watten	KW1 5XN Dunn Farm
49	Achavanich	KW5 6DX farm
50	Rangag	KW5 6DX farm
22	Latheron	KW5 6DG farm
21	Lybster	KW3 6AE main street

PART FOUR: Saints and Sources

'Now there were dwelling in Jerusalem Jews, devout men from every nation under heaven. And at this sound the multitude came together, and they were bewildered, because each one heard them speaking in his own language. And they were amazed and wondered, saying, 'Are not all these who are speaking Galileans? And how is it that we hear, each of us in his own native language? Parthians, Medes and Elomites; residents of Mesopotamia, Judea and Cappadocia, Pontus and Asia, Phrygia and Pamphylia, Egypt and the parts of Lybia belonging to Cyrene, and visitors from Rome, both Jews and proselytes , Cretans and Arabians, we hear them telling in our own tongues the mighty works of God. (Acts 2:5-11)

Alphabetical List of Saints

The naming of saints is not always obvious. The local names were of Pictish or Celtic origin but were often only written down in Latin, perhaps hundreds of years after the life being described. Later, Gaelic and English were used. To add to the confusion, some saints changed their names, as do some modern monks and nuns. Also, the same name was often repeated through the generations and it can be difficult to work out who was who. So the following is sometimes a 'best guess'. Also, you will notice that the descriptions include many examples of 'possibly'; 'almost certainly'; 'it is assumed that' and similar phrases. This reflects the scarcity of verifiable source material but also reflects the feel for the subject acquired through reading the opinions of scholars who have devoted their lives to piecing together what information is available.

This list only names those saints that have a connection with the places named on the Northern Pilgrims' Way and the Northern Saints Trails.

My sources have themselves relied heavily on the Aberdeen Breviary, the first printed book to be produced in Scotland. It was compiled by Bishop William Elphinstone of Aberdeen and produced in 1510. The Breviary contained biographies of all known Scottish saints, with prayers to be used on their feast days and various other liturgical texts. As with so many other things, the bishop's motives were both religious and political – by bringing together all this material, the bishop was demonstrating to the world, and to the Pope in particular, that Scotland was an independent country, with its own history and culture. Sadly, with the Reformation ban on venerating saints, the Breviary became obsolete and is now only available to those with access to rare academic books.

Anne 1st C; Feast Day: 26th July

There is only one reference to Anne, the maternal grandmother of Jesus. 'According to Sir John R. G. Sinclair, Bart. of Dunbeath, the church at Dunnet was dedicated to St Anne'[53]. There is no hint as to why Sir John said this. It is more likely that the Dunnet church was dedicated to Mary as the local summer fair is called the Marymas Fair and, until recently, was held on the first Saturday after the 15th August – the feast of the Assumption of Our Lady.

Adamnan (d.704) Feast Day: 23rd September

Adamnan was brought up in Donegal. He was the abbot of Iona apr 100 years after Columba and is most famous for his biography of Columba. He travelled between Scotland and Ireland regularly. He is associated with many places in the central belt, east coast and western islands. In the north, he is remembered in Inverness, Abriachan, Glen Urquhart (where there is a chapel and croft dedicated to him) and Damsey Island in Orkney. In Glen Lyon, people still tell the story of how Adamnan stopped a plague from spreading by planting his crozier at Craigianie. Nearby, on a small knoll, *Tom a' Mhoid* 'the moot-knoll', is a small stone with a cross carved on it. Adamnan supported the reforms agreed at Whitby.

See Towill p. 1; MacQuarrie p. 160; Woodside p 39; Watson p. 270.

---

[53] See Eccl Hist p. 315.

Andrew 1st century. Feast day: 30th November

Dedications to Andrew are more common in the central belt and southern areas than in the Highlands. He superseded Malie as patron saint of the parish of Golspie. (Malie may be a corruption of Maelrubha – see the entry for Malie below.)

See Towill p. 10; Cat p 36.

Barr – see Finbar

Benedict 480-547. Feast day: 11th July

Two of my sources give 'Benedict' as the dedication for a site at Shurrery. However, this is almost certainly a mis-translation of the Latin *Benediction* – a blessing, giving the site the name 'House of Blessing'. There is now nothing to be seen at the Shurrery site (ND 0405 5785) but there was once a chapel, graveyard and simple carved slab with a circle and equal-armed cross, dated to the seventh or eighth century. This early date, well before the Benedictine order reached Scotland, also argues against a dedication to Benedict. The carved slab is now at Sandside House, Reay.

Benedict was the founding abbot of the monastery of Subiaco, a few miles outside Rome, for about twenty-five years. During that time, he wrote The Rule of Saint Benedict. This is a deceptively short and mundane set of rules governing daily life in the monastery that has become the standard by which thousands of monks and lay people from then to now order their lives. The Benedictine Rule with its order of monks gradually spread through Europe, arriving in

Scotland with the support of Queen Margaret in 1070. The two most northerly Benedictine monasteries were Beauly Priory and Pluscarden Abbey, both far removed from Caithness. As these monks did not travel far from their own monasteries, it seems unlikely that there was a connection with Shurrery. Beauly priory is a ruin but Pluscarden Abbey, having fallen into a ruin after the Reformation, has been restored and is now the oldest monastic building being used for its original purpose in Britain.

See Cat p. 37, Eccl Hist p 39, 315, 333.

Bridget (c. 451 – 525). Feast day 1ˢᵗ February

A heap of stones about 100 yards from Achscorrieclett, on the Eastern shore of Loch More mark the remains of a chapel dedicated to Bridget. There is also a holy well to the NNW of the stones. Bridget is also commemorated on the Orkney islands of Stronsay and Papa Stronsay.

There are several Brides, Brigits, Bridhdes, which could be pagan goddesses or historical figures. The most famous is Bridget of Kildare. There are dedications to Bridget all over Scotland, especially around the Solway, where they probably. refer to the Irish Bridget. Those in the Highlands and Islands, where there is the most folk-lore associated with the name, may be referring to a local figure as Bride is a Pictish name (Brude being the male version).

See Towill p. 29; Cat p. 31; Ecc Hist p. 62, 313; Inv. no. 168.

Catherine/ Katherine 14th and 4th centuries.

Feast Days 29th April and 25th November

There was a convent and well at Murkle, close to the shore, referred to as Cloisters by the locals and near a place later called Redland's well. There was also a monastery on the south side of the bay at Murkle House. Murkle was an important political site, possibly because of these religious houses – Earl John of Caithness gave his oath to a representative of King Edward 1 of England there in 1296 and Earl Arnfinn died there, possibly on the orders of his wife, Ragnhild.[54] Another joint convent, well and monastery dedicated to Katherine lay to the west of the manse at Watten. There is a chapel and graveyard dedicated to Katherine at Gerston, on the outskirts of Halkirk (ND 1224 59350 and possibly at the Sibster Burn near Georgemas Junction station (ND 1507 5959). Some sources also mention a chapel dedicated to Katherine near the bishop's palace in Halkirk, near Quoycrook (ND 1299 5900). There are no visible remains at any of these sites.

Catherine of Siena and Katherine of Alexandria both have their main centres in Edinburgh – Catherine in the area of Sciennes and Katherine at Roscobie but with other dedications throughout the country. As Catherine of Siena is a 14th century saint and 'our' saints pre-date this, they must refer to Katherine of Alexandria, who was martyred in the 4th century and after whom the Catherine Wheel is named as she was burned to death strapped to a cart wheel.

---

[54] See Crawford p.112 and p. 311.

For details of the link between Katherine of Alexandria and the Sinclair family of both Rosslyn and Caithness, go to the section on the village of Watten in Part Two.

See Towill p. 120; Cat p. 37; Ecc Hist p. 44, 45, 57, 60, 334; Inv no. 490, 491.

Ciaran (d. 549/617/618). Feast day 9th Sept

Ciaran was a follower of Donan and was one of the Eigg martyrs (see under Donan). He founded chapels and burial grounds at Strathmore and Dalnawillan, Caithness. The Dalnawillan site is close to the upper reaches of the Thurso River, near where the Glutt and Rumsdale Rivers join it. He is also associated with the site at Rangag where the remains of a broch or castle can be seen from the road, and Latheron, where there was a chapel near the shore and a carved cross (see under 'Latheron' in Part One). There are dedications to him on Lewis, in many sites along the west coast and in the east at Loch Tay.

See Cat p. 33; Woodside p. 50; Ecc Hist p. 62; Inv no. 176; Watson p. 278.

Clement (d. c.100). Feast day 23rd November

There is a link between Clement and Danish seafarers, as this dedication is found in several fishing towns on the east coast which had trading links with Denmark in the early Middle Ages (including East Anglia, where there are painted screens depicting him). This suggest that the Clement in question is the

172

4th bishop of Rome as he is said to have been killed by being thrown into the sea with an anchor round his neck and angels then made a tomb for his body on the sea bed. Clement is the patron saint of Dingwall, which was a trading post for Danish seafarers and whose name has Viking links.

Colman (7th century). Feast day 18th February

Colman is a very common name throughout Scotland, Ireland and England. Here I refer to the Colman who was a monk on Iona before becoming the 3rd bishop of Lindisfarne. After the Synod of Whitby, he resigned rather than accept the new dates for Easter. He returned to Iona and then went to Tarbet, Easter Ross where he built a chapel dedicated to S Aidan. This was later changed to his own name. He is also linked with Kintyre and Caithness, where he founded a chapel at Old Reay close to the sea. He is linked to the Reay parish church that was in use until 1739. The Kyle of Sutherland has the remains of a chapel and graveyard at Kilmachalmaig, which may refer to him. He may be buried at Portmahomack, whose name means 'Colman's Port'.

Just to confuse matters, some sources list a Colman as one of Donnan's followers from Kildonan, much closer to Reay than the other sites associated with the name. So we may be talking of two Colmans here.

The site at Reay is easily accessible from the main road, to the left as you travel westwards and just past the primary school on the right. There are no longer remains of Colman's chapel but another church was built in the 16th century on the site and was used until the new church was built in 1739. There is a graveyard and mausoleum. The mausoleum was used by the MacKay's of Bighouse. It has a carved stone built into the wall. For further details and a photograph, see https://highlandpictishtrail.co.uk/project/reay-cross-slab/

See Towill p. 40; Woodside p. 58; Ecc Hist p. 39, 80; Watson p. 278.

Colum (?6th C)

There is much confusion over who is being referred to here as some sources assume that 'Colum' is a corruption of 'Columba' or 'Colman' or even 'Coomb'. However there was a Colum who worked on Orkney, so the sites at Dunnet Links and Olrig (St Coomb), and Dirlot may well have originally been founded by Colum. The Dirlot dedication is sometimes listed as 'Columba' but this is almost certainly a misunderstanding by writers who were not familiar with the early Celtic saints and Colm/Colum is far more likely.

See Cat p. 35; Ecc Hist p. 83.

Columba/Columcille (d.597). Feast day 9th June

Columba was probably born in 521 and came to Iona in 563 or soon after. He studied under St Finnian. He may have founded the monasteries at Durrow and Derry. He was a political exile as much as a religious

174

one and continued to be involved in politics at some level in both Ireland and Scotland, returning to Ireland several times. He visited King Bridei at his fortress at Craig Phatric, Inverness, when he asked for safe passage for Cormac who was seeking a hermitage, possibly on Orkney, and for others of his followers.

Dedications to Columba occur in several places north of the Great Glen. Some of these dedications may be to sites founded by his followers, others may be to saints with similar-sounding names. The so-called Columban monasteries and communities along the Moray Firth may be attributed to St Colm of Buchan, one of 'The Drostan Three'. Other sites include Eilean nan Naomh, (Isle of Saints, off the mouth of the Naver), where there was a monastery; Rig of Columba at Skerray on the mainland opposite the above island; a chapel and well at Dirlot, as there is a well near the shepherd's house called *Tobar Choluim-Cille* (well of Columba), (but see 'Colum' above); a chapel and well at Kilchalumkil, Strathbrora, Clyne and *Clachan Chollumchille* in Invermoriston. His followers spread throughout the country.

See Towill p. 42; Cat p. 33; Woodhouse p. 17; MacQuarrie p. 74; Ecc Hist p. 62, 83, 314, 335; Inv no. 169, 170.

Comgan (pr. Cowan)/Congan/Coan/Cowan
(8th century) Feast day 13th Oct

Comgan ruled as a prince in Leinster for a few years. He came to Scotland with his widowed sister,

Kentigerna, and her son, Filian. They settled in the Lochalsh area, where his nephew built a church in his honour. He then moved to Turriff but was buried on Iona. Dedications include Kilchowan in Kiltearn (Ross and Cromarty); Kilchoan or Kilcongan (Isle of Seil); St Coan in Strath (Skye); Kilchoan, Ardnamurachan and Knoydart; the Kilchoan estate where there is a very ancient ruined church dedicated to St Comgan.

See Towill p. 51; Woodside p. 63.

Coomb/Colm (? 6th century).

While some dedications to Coomb/Colm are assumed to be to Columba, they are more likely to be to either St Colum/Coomb of Orkney or Colm of Buchan, a follower of Drostan. A site which seems to be associated with Colm is that near the Burn of Mid-sands, Dunnet, also called Links of Old Tain. This site was buried under sand during a storm (see the entry for Dunnet Links in Part Three). When the Links road was being built it was slightly turned to avoid the site. Later, a local contractor quarrying sand in the area uncovered human remains, suggesting that there had been a graveyard beside the chapel. The quarrying was discontinued.

See Ecc Hist p. 45, 83, 314, 333; Inv no. 331.

Cormack

The Gaelic source of the name (corbmac) translates as 'chariot-lad'. Various placenames derive from Cormac – two Balcormocks, one near Abercrombie and one near Lundie, Fife, both now known as Balcormo, Another Balvormo can be found in Forfar. Whether or not these places were dedicated to 'our' Cormack is now impossible to tell. The Cormack that we are interested in may have been a follower of either Columba or Adamnon, as both are credited with persuading King Brude to give Cormack the regulus of Orkney. He may have settled on Colme Isle (Eilean nan Naomh) at the mouth of the Naver River and dedicated it to Columba.

See Cat p. 40-41; Watson p.237.

Curitan/Boniface (c. 7th century). Feast day16[th] March

Curitan had been sent north from Wearmouth Abbey to help King Nechtan establish Roman customs (he was a Pict). He is mentioned in the literature as both bishop and abbot. He worked around Invergowrie, Perth, Forfar then moved to Rosemarkie, on the Black Isle, north of Inverness. Curitan had the religious name 'Boniface'. Just as he had changed his own name, so he did not hesitate to change the names of chapels dedicated to the early Celtic saints. His favourite dedication was to Peter as there was a family tradition that they were descended from Peter's sister, Radia. He built a chapel dedicated to Peter at Rosemarkie. Many miracles there are attributed to him. When he was ordained a bishop, he built his cathedral at Fortrose. Dedications include Glen Urquhart, Avoch, in a fair at Loth called Carden and perhaps at Eyartan in Braemore, Latheron.

See Towill p. 57; Cat p. 36; Woodside p. 48; Watson p. 315.

Cuthbert (7th century), Feast day 20th March

Cuthbert came from the borders and is best known as the Abbot of Lindisfarne. There is one chapel and graveyard dedicated to him in Caithness. It lies 200 yards ESE of Upper Haster farm house at the lower end of a cultivated field on the Burn of Haster and about 100 yards W of the Achairn burn.

See Towill p. 61; Cat p. 37; Ecc Hist p. 56, 315, Inv no. 593; Watson p. 315.

Devenic (6th century). Feast day 13th Nov

Devenick was a contemporary of Columba and Machar. He is mainly associated with the Don and the Dee river valleys in Aberdeenshire and he founded two churches at Methlick and at Lower Banchory or Banchory-Devenick. He also travelled around Caithness, where he died in 877. His remains were taken to Banchory-Devenick for burial, where he is the patron saint. There is also a connection to a fair at Creich, Sutherland.

See Towill p. 61; Cat p. 37; Woodside p. 14; L of N issue 6.

Diman (7th century).

Diman was named in a letter of Pope-elect John in 640 regarding the controversy over the dating

178

of Easter. He was associated with Daimsey, Orkney but died in Strathnaver in 670.

See Cat p. 35.

Donan/Donnan (d. 617). Feast day 17th April

Donan was one of the most important figures in early Church history in the Highlands. He was probably Irish and a contemporary of Columba. He seems to have started his Scottish mission at Whithorn, Ninian's base, and gradually moved north via Arran and Iona. He eventually settled with his followers at Suisgill, Kildonan on the Helmsdale River. His community founded eight churches, including Fordyce in Banffshire (Talorcan), Reay (Colman), Halkirk (Tarlogan), and Strathmore in Caithness (Ciaran). He is also commemorated at Auchterless, Aberdeenshire, where his 'bachail' or staff was kept. There are many 'Kildonan's up the West coast e.g. the site of the famous castle at Eilean Donan on Lochalsh, Cil Donan (Loch Garry). Donan and many of his followers moved from Kildonan to Eigg, where their settlement also became known as Kildonan. In 617, 52 of them were martyred. There are conflicting stories of the martyrdom but the most popular is that they were trapped in a cave while saying Mass and were burned to death by Viking raiders. This is probably not historically accurate, as the Viking raids were typically late 8th century and after. Iona Abbey was first plundered in 794. A more likely story is that the instigator of the burning was a powerful local lady who took exception to them cultivating her ground as she had been used to grazing her cattle on it. So she encouraged some local pirates to kill the monks in return for any valuables that they might find there. The usual date quoted is Easter Sunday 17th April 617 AD.

The community later re-established itself under the leadership of the Iona monks. A cave on the island is known as the cathedral cave but it is not clear whether this is because it was the one used for saying Mass or because of its shape.

See Towill p. 70; Cat p. 33, 40, 51; Woodside p. 50; Ecc Hist pp. 78-82; Scott 'St Donnan the Great and his Muinntir'.

Drostan (c. 6th century). Feast day 14th December

Drostan is a Pictish name. It appears in many forms – Trostan, Tristan, Tustan, Trothan, Tear and Tear, Teer, Tustimas, Trothermass. (The mutation of D to T and vice-versa is common to both Pictish and Old Welsh usage). According to some sources, Drostan is said to be the son of a friend of St Columba, Aidan of Dalriada. He was sent to Columba in Ireland to be educated and became a monk there. According to other sources, Drostan was the son of a Welsh prince and the uncle, through his sister, of Aedhan/Aidan. This second theory would make him older than Columba and unlikely to have studied under him.

Drostan is associated with many places in Aberdeenshire and the North East, also in Glen Urquhart, Galloway and Fife. He was the first abbot, possibly the founder, of the monastic institution at Deer in Buchan. The monastery was founded some time between 563 and 597. According to the Book of Deer, Columba taught Drostan at Deer but this is disputed. Other claims that Columba came to the area with Drostan to negotiate for a site for an abbey at Aberdour are also debated. His bones are in a stone tomb in Aberdour. Some sources claim that he was 'gaelicised' and made to be subordinate to Columba for political reasons.

Note: Columba's foundations at Derry and Durrow both derive their names from the same Gaelic source as Deer. If Deer was deliberately named after Durrow (which also produced famous books), this may explain the Columban connection.

Drostan's followers in Caithness, where he was known as Trostan, were Fergus, Colum/Colm and Modan/Madan. The Chapel of Teer, at Shorelands near Ackergill, is connected with Deer in Aberdeenshire. Teer is a Caithness form of Deer, even as Trostan is of Drostan. The abbot of Deer had lands and tenants in Caithness, which may have been gifted from the Keiths of Ackergill, whose original home was near Deer. This chapel was linked with the Feast of the Holy Innocents, presumably because of the association between its name and the tears shed by the families of the babies killed by King Herod. Local people would gather at the chapel on the feast day of the Holy Innocents (usually the third day after Christmas) and offer up gifts of bread and cheese. The day would turn into a social event, with pipers playing for dances. This tradition took many decades to die out after the Reformation, despite the best efforts of the local ministers.

There is a story of a local shepherd, not wanting to see good food going to waste, removing the offerings once the people had gone home and feeding them to his dogs.

An aside about the Chapel of Teer: in a clan dispute between the Gunns and the Keiths, it was agreed to meet to settle the matter at the chapel of Teer, near Wick. The Keiths cheated and murdered the Gunns. This must have happened after 1461. (See Cat p. 103.)

Dedications to Drostan occur at various sites around Caithness. At Westfield, on the 'back road' from Thurso to Reay there was a chapel to the east of the burial ground. The baptismal font is on the south wall of the burial ground. Westerdale, has two sites. Between Olgrinmore and Westerdale is a burial ground and chapel, opposite a place called Aisle. A little further to the NW is St Trostan's well. There is also a chapel and unenclosed graveyard at the edge of a field to the E of the road that leads from Westerdale to Balindannich and ½ m N of the former place. Then there is Chapel Field at Lyth, just to the east of Barrock House.

The site with the most history attached is Olrig, on the southerly edge of the village of Castletown. Tucked in behind the modern graveyard, is a very old graveyard with the ruins of the parish church of Olrig known as St Trothan's at the entrance. It is said to have been erected in 1643 and used as the parish church until 1840. Here the market day of

Tustimas /Trothermas was held on the fourth Tuesday in November right up to 1902. A socketed plinth of an ancient churchyard cross is on the south side of the building and marks a spot called the Witches' grave in some records and the Selkie's grave in others. 'Selkie' is the local word for a seal/woman who can appear to be an ordinary woman by casting off her seal skin but returns to being a seal when she puts it on again. There are many legends of selkies who either adopted human form, married and had children or enticed men into a watery grave or prison. The Olrig selkie was found on the shore as a baby wrapped in a sealskin. Her finder, a local fisherman, took her home to his wife and they raised her as their own. Some versions say that she married their son. All agree that she was banished from the kirk, possibly because she claimed to have seen the devil or because she seemed to have unnatural powers, hence the 'Witches grave'. She died in childbirth. Her grave never dries out.

There was a nunnery in what is now a field on the other side of the road. There are no remains to be seen.

The present church at Canisbay is on the site of a church dedicated to Drostan; inland, at Brabstermire on the W side of the high road to the NW of Brabstermire House is another chapel (ND 317 694). The baptismal font is in Brabster House.

See Towill p. 73; Cat p. 35, 42, 103; Woodside p. 20; Inventory no 57, 159, 167, 175, 317; Ecc Hist p. 45, 49, 51, 58, 62, 82; Watson p. 333; CFC issue 1987; Scott 'St Drostan of Buchan and Caithness'.

Duthac (11th century). feast day 8th March

The name 'Duthac' is seldom mentioned outside the town of Tain, which was his birthplace around the year 1000. Yet, in his lifetime and for several hundred years after, Duthac was one of the most important saints of Scotland. People flocked to Tain in his lifetime to hear him preach or to pray for a cure of an illness, and indeed he was a renowned miracle-worker. He trained as a priest in Ireland, gaining the title of Confessor of Ireland and Scotland, and travelled between there and Tain regularly, eventually dying there in 1065. In 1253 his relics, consisting of his head, a breastbone and a 'hairy shirt' were returned to Tain and the Collegiate Church was built to house them. Sadly, these were lost at the Reformation, although the statue of him remained – so precious to the townspeople that they refused to destroy it. The only known painting of Duthac is a small wall-painting in Cologne Cathedral, dated to around 1320. He is also mentioned in the Martyrology of Cologne, printed in 1490. It is not clear what the connection between Cologne and Duthac was. Perhaps the cathedral was a popular destination for Scottish pilgrims as it housed the relics of the three Magi/kings of Christmas Carol fame?

Evidence of Duthac's connections to the West coast exist in place names such as Loch Duich in Kintail. The modern RC church in Dornie on the shores of Loch Duich is dedicated to St Duthac. (On the shores of Loch Duich is Eilean Donnan Castle, a clear dedication to another of 'our' saints.) He is also honoured as far south as Galloway and Ayrshire. In

Caithness, St Duthac's (or St Duddock's) chapel was built on some raised ground near the Burn of Kirk Stanes on Killimster Moss, about 1 mile to the west of Loch Killimster. There had been a lull in Christian missionary work in the north due to Viking raids. The work of Duthac and his community (the site is thought to be monastic, not just a solitary chapel) in the area marked a revival and devotion to him continued well into the post-Reformation times. There was a tradition of people from Wick and Mirelandhall visiting the site on Christmas day before sunrise to leave gifts of bread, cheese and a silver coin on a stone in the middle of the Burn of Killimster. This tradition continued into the early 19th century. A fair used to be held at Killimster on the first Tuesday in March.

'But what about Orkney?', I hear you ask. Well, we know that Duthac had a large following on Orkney as there was an ancient chapel dedicated to him at Sandwick and, when the cathedral was built, the main side-altar was dedicated to him. We even know from estate papers that this was maintained by an annual stipend from Doehouse Farm, Sandwick. In 1448 Earl William Sinclair founded a chapel dedicated to Duthac at Pickaquoy, just outside Kirkwall. By 1903, the site had become a quarry and by 1964 it is described on maps as a recreation ground. Today, it is part of Kirkwall and has the town's leisure centre on it. It is possible that Magnus himself was one of Duthac's followers, as local tradition says that the chapel at Spittal, Caithness on the pilgrimage route to

Tain was founded by Magnus.[55] Another local tradition says that the chapel, known as St Magnus' Chapel, was so called because it was used by pilgrims on their way to St Magnus Cathedral, Kirkwall. Both traditions could be true.

The Aberdeen Breviary (1510) gives us a picture of Duthac as a very practical man, who cared for people's basic needs such as food, shelter and good health. He also had a reputation for finding lost articles – a Scottish version of St Anthony!

In their day, Duthac was better known than Magnus, our other 'destination' saint. However, partly due to the Cathedral built by his nephew, Rognvald, the cult of Magnus (d. 1117) grew and the cathedral became a popular pilgrimage centre. The three places in Caithness linked with his name will be described as we journey north. The cult of Duthac gradually dwindled after the Reformed churches banned pilgrimages and the veneration of saints. Also, Tain no longer enjoyed royal patronage or political influence. However there are signs that Duthac may be becoming better known again. The modern St Duthac's Way runs from Tain to St Andrew's via Aberdeen. There is also the beginnings of a 'St Duthac's Way' from the head of Loch Duich, Kintail through Glen Affric towards, but not quite reaching, Tain.

---

[55] See the leaflets produced by the Spittal Hall Committee, listed in the Bibliography under 'Sinclair, A.'

See Watson p.284; Towill p. 75; Cat p. 36; Woodside p. 83; Ecc Hist p. 50, 83; Inventory no 592.

Erchard/Irchard/Yrchard/Merchard (5th century). Feast day 24th August

Erchard was a Pictish bishop of the 5th century. He was born in Kincardine O'Neill and studied under St Ternan at Banchory. He travelled with two companions to the Great Glen and Strathglass, where he found three bells (some sources say that they were found at Dunbeath). Erchard then settled in Glen Morriston, where one of the bells survived into more modern times. Local tradition is that it could float on water but there was an injunction on anyone putting this to the test for a wager. He travelled to Rome and was made a bishop by Pope St Gregory.

See Woodside p. 11.

Ernan (d.617/618)

A chapel and burial ground in the Strath of Kildonan are dedicated to Ernan. He was one of the 52 followers of Donnan who were martyred on Eigg. There is also a Killearnan on the Black Isle.

See Cat p. 33.

Faolan/Fillan

The name means 'little wolf'. He has a dedication in the parish church at Clyne. He may be the son of Kentigerna and nephew of Comgan. Local tradition says that he is buried at Cill Fhaolain, Kilillan, in Kintail. He is the saint of Loch Alsh, while Kentigerna's cell is on the south side of Loch Duich. He is also associated with Loch Earn Head.

See Cat p. 32; Watson p. 284.

Fergus (6[th,] 7th or 8th century). Feast day 18th Nov
He is the patron saint of Wick but is also remembered in Halkirk. The knoll at Halkirk on which St Fergus church stands was previously known as Tore Harlogan, indicating an earlier dedication to Talorc/ Tarloc/Tarlogan, another follower of Donan. These two names are also linked in Banffshire. For more details of Fergus and Wick, see the entry on Wick in Part Three.

Fergus is associated with the North-East and with Drostan (6th C), Medan and Colm. He is also associated with Donnan (d. 617) and his name is on the Tallagh list. This is a Pictish name and dedications cover almost exactly the same area as the great Pictish stones. He seems to have spent time in Ireland, where he had the. status of a bishop, then Strathearn, then Caithness, then Buchan.

Other dedications occur at Moy (Inverness-shire), also in Wigtownshire and Dundee (but there was another Fergus, or Fergustus, a Pictish bishop who attended a council in Rome in 721. This Fergus was described as 'Fergus a Pict, a bishop of Scotia' meaning that he came from the north of Scotland but was a bishop in Ireland)[56].

St Fergus supported the reforms agreed at the Synod of Whitby.

See Cat p. 36, 43; Towill p. 86; Woodside p. 65; Inventory no. 493, 582; Ecc Hist p. 5, 54, 9, 81, 314, 334.

Finian/Finbar/Barr/Finnian (d.579)

Finbarr's name has many variants. '*Finnian* is the first half of the name loaded with the diminutive of endearment or honour. The full name *Finbarr* was used both in Caithness and Sutherland. When the name was halved in conversation, the latter half was nearly always preferred in these districts.'[57]

The sources suggest that there were two saints of the same name, both associated with Ninian and Whithorn. One was born in Ulster and was educated at Candida Casa. He returned to Ireland, where he taught Columba. In the south, his name becomes Winning, Wynnian, Barr. In the north, his name becomes Fymbar or St Barr. It may have been his psalter that Columba copied without permission, leading to Columba's move to Iona.

The other Finbar may have been born on the

---

[56] Watson, p. 322

[57] As quoted in 'Chapters in the History of the Church of the Picts (II) – S. Finbarr of Caithness and Ulster' Transactions of the Gaelic Society of Inverness 6.2.1908

banks of the Berriedale Water (previously called Bardale or Berudal and translated as Barr's valley) not very far from the high road that runs between Helmsdale and Wick. According to Rev A. B. Scott, it is possible that this Finbar could have been related to the leading families of both Caithness and Ulster as there was much inter-marrying between them and Finbar's prominence suggests that he came from a powerful family. He trained in the north, possibly at Ninian's House, Edderton. (Other sources suggest that he trained at Candida Casa, Whithorn, but this may be a confusion with the Irish Finbar.) He founded a church at Dornoch adjacent to the modern cathedral where his fair was held on 25th September (This was later changed to 10th October and again to 25th October). He also founded a church in Caithness, probably at Barrock where local tradition is that a field known as 'chapel field' had a chapel dedicated to Saint Barr.

The name 'Achvarasdal', where there is a well-known broch, means Barr's valley.

When Gilbert built his cathedral in Dornoch, he dedicated it to Finbarr (some sources say that the dedication was to Mary and, on his death, it was changed to St Gilbert and Mary). There seems to have been a strong cult of St Finbarr in the Dornoch area at that time. A royal charter from King David gives the monks based there protection in their travels through Caithness and Orkney.[58] Devotion to Finbarr continued into the 16th century as Chapel Barr at Mid-

---

[58] See Crawford p. 185

Geanies in Ross-shire is thought to have been built by Abbot Thomas of Fearn Abbey (1486-1516).

Folk memory of Finbarr lingered on into the 19th Century and Rev A.B. Scott recounts a story given to him by Sir John Sinclair who attended a meeting in Thurso to discuss building a new church. A member of the group suggested that this church should be called after Finbar as he had been a much-venerated teacher in Caithness and beyond. No one else at the meeting had heard of him and the suggestion was ignored.

See Cat p. 40; Towill p. 94; Ecc Hist p. 66, 73-78, 334; Scott 'Chapters in the History of the Church of the Picts (II)'.

Fion

Cill Fhinn or Killin occurs in various places and suggests a Saint Fion, although none appears on the various lists. On the Northern Pilgrims' Way, the name is associated with Loch Garve in Ross-shire and Loch Brora in Sutherland.

Francis (12th century). Feast day 4th October

A convent at Dornoch and a nunnery at Cloisters, Wick are dedicated to Francis. This could be Francis of Assisi, founder of the Franciscan order, whose followers came to England in 1224. The order spread rapidly throughout the country and devotees may well have reached the far north. The site of the nunnery is not marked on the maps but was most likely to have been at Mount Hooley. The site of the nunnery at Murkle is also named 'Cloisters' and it is possible that this is simply an alternative name for 'nunnery' rather than a geographical location.

See Cat p. 37.

Fumac (c. 6th century). Feast day 3rd May

He is associated mainly with Keith, Banffshire but also at St Fumac's Fair at Dinet and at Chapel of Dine, both on the outskirts of Watten, Caithness.

See Woodside p. 35.

Gavin (4th century).

The only recorded saint of this name was an early Christian martyr, an ex Roman centurion, decapitated in 300 AD and whose head was thrown in the Mediterranean Sea before being reunited with his body. There are no known links between him and Caithness.

About ¼ m SE of Dorrery Lodge and within an enclosed graveyard are the ruins of a small chapel called Gavin's Kirk or Temple Gavin. The surrounding land once belonged to the bishops of Caithness. As the land around the graveyard once belonged to the bishops of Orkney and there was a Bishop Gavin in Orkney at one point, it is likely that this is the Gavin referred to.

See Cat p. 37; Ecc Hist p. 61; Inventory no 90.

George (4th century). Feast day 23rd April

George is associated with Palestine. He may have been a soldier and was probably martyred during the persecutions of Diocletian. Devotion to him flourished during the Crusades after a vision of him was seen just before an important victory during the 1st crusade.

None of the lists of local saints mention George but there was a Georgemas Fair near the site of Georgemas Junction railway station. See the information on Spittal in Part Two for some ideas on how the fair got this name.

Gilbert (d. 1245). Feast day 1st April

Gilbert started his priestly life in Moray. He may have encouraged the cult of St Duthac of Tain and himself worked many miracles. He succeeded Bishop Adam, who had been murdered, as bishop of Caithness in 1222/3. He built an episcopal palace at Burnside, Thurso, St Peter's Kirk near-by and the cathedral at Dornoch, which was dedicated to St Finbarr (This may be a confusion between the actual dedication to Mary and the nearby original chapel and graveyard dedicated to Finbarr). Gilbert had been given large tracts of Sutherland by a relative as a personal gift and presumably felt safer here than in the rebellious north. The bones of the murdered Bishop Adam were taken to the cathedral in 1239. Gilbert was an excellent administrator and set up a complex system of diocesan administration as well as dividing his diocese into parishes.[59]. A comment in Woodside[60] that 'he is reputed to have civilised Caithness' probably refers to this organisation of the area rather than any civic influence. A century after Gilbert's death in 1245, Dornoch Cathedral was re-dedicated to 'Saint Mary and Saint Gilbert'.

See Cat p. 73, 81; Woodside p. 90, 91.

Ian (d. 617/618)

Ian was a disciple of Donan and was martyred on Eigg. Dedications occur in the church of Kilean, Strathbrora, Clyne and in a well near Helmsdale. Other dedications in Helmsdale to John, including another well, may refer to this Ian as Ian is the Gaelic version of John and Donan's centre before moving to Eigg was up-river from Helmsdale. However by the 14th century, the church and well in Helmsdale were both referred to as of 'John the Baptist'.

See Cat p. 34.

James (1st century). Feast day 25th July

It is assumed that this James is the apostle, 'James, the brother of John'. An altar in Dornoch Cathedral and a fair (*Lafeill Sheamuis* or Jamesmas) are dedicated to James.

See Cat p. 36.

---

[59] See Crawford p. 267
[60] Woodside, p.91

John (1st century). Feast day 27th December (the apostle) or 29th August (the Baptist)

The Gaelic form of the name is Killean. It is not always clear whether the dedication refers to John the Baptist or John the apostle. Festivals at midsummer (24 June) or 29 August suggest John the Baptist. Local tradition in Dunnet is that St John's Loch is so called after the Baptist as its waters were used for baptisms. The name is associated with Urquhart, Perth, Kirkcudbright, Edinburgh, the high cross on Iona and Cheyne in Sutherland. The knights of St John of Jerusalem (Hospitallers) had a chapel dedicated to John in Inverness.

Caithness and Sutherland dedications exist in Dunnet, St John's Head and Helmsdale. Near the east shore of St John's Loch, Dunnet there can just be made out the foundation marks of a chapel and graveyard. Local tradition is that unbaptised babies were buried in the graveyard. There was also a tradition where the sick would walk round the loch before sunrise on the first Mondays of May, August, November and February, bath in it and throw a coin in. Another version is that the sick would walk round the loch three times on mid-summer's morning before dawn.

The St John's Head site, to the east of Dunnet Head was once protected by a moat and dyke. There is some evidence of a stone cist inside a wall but its original purpose is unclear.

On Dunnet Head, at Chapel Geo, there can still be seen the remains of a hermit's chapel and cell but no name is associated with the site.

The Helmsdale dedications are on the site of the existing Church of Scotland and the well on the opposite side of the river to the church.

See Cat p. 37; Ecc Hist p. 46, p 48; Inv no. 56, 79, 88; Towill p. 113, 116.

Katherine/Katherine of Alexandria
See under 'Catherine'.

Kenneth (6th century)
Kenneth was born in Derry about 525 and studied in Wales. He was a companion of Columba and went with him to King Brude in Inverness. There are many dedications to him, particularly in Fife.

See Towill p. 125.

Kentigerna (d.734) feast day 7th January
Kentigerna has been mentioned earlier as the sister of Comgan and mother of Faolan. She was the daughter of Cellach Cualan of Leinster. She is associated with Loch Duich, where her chapel was at *cill Chaointeord* or Kilchintorn on the south side of the loch. She also lived as an anchorite on the island on Loch Lomond called Inch Cailleach, 'the nun's isle'. She died there and the church is dedicated to her.

See Watson p.301.

Kessog (6th century) Feast day 10th March

Kessog (sometimes written 'Cessoc') was Irish. He worked in what is now East Dunbartonshire, mainly around Loch Lomond and Callander. He retired to Monk's Island on Loch Lomond.

There are two sites dedicated to him near Inverness – North and South Kessock. The South Kessock ferry (run by Dominican monks) to North Kessock was used by pilgrims going to Tain. This ferry was replaced by a bridge in 1982, called the Kessock Bridge.

An aside – the Highland surname 'MacIsaac', which is also found around Callander, may be a corruption of Kessog.

See Towill p. 138; Woodside p. 27.

Madan

This may, or may not, be Modan/Medan, the companion of Drostan. If not, he may be associated with Bowermadden. Some sources link the site at Bowernadden with Drostan, suggesting that Madden is indeed Modan/Medan one of Drostan's three companions.

See Cat p. 35; Ecc Hist p. 49.

Maelrubha (b. 3 Jan 642). Feast day 21st April

Maelrubha, (*Sagairt Ruadh* , the red priest) was born in Derry in 642 and came to Applecross in 671. He was a contemporary of Adamnon. There are many variations on his name, including ones that

197

could be mistaken for Mary, for example Maree. Many dedications exist, including Urquhart, Forres, Fordyce, Keith, Contin, Arisaig, Gairloch, Loch Maree, Portree, Lochcarron, Lairg, Durness, Farr. His main base was in Applecross, where he was the abbot of a monastery for 50 years. In the same area is Loch Maree with a small island 'Innis Maree' which has a ruined chapel, graveyard, holy well and an oak tree studded with nails. Further north, as the coastline turns eastward, is Balnakeil and a ruined chapel founded by Maelrubha in 722. The Murie Fair at Lairg was held on Maelrubha's feast day. Contin also had a church and fair dedicated to him. The fair later moved to Dingwall.

There was a legend that he was killed by Vikings in Glen Urquhart. This has been discounted and the current belief is that he was killed by Danes, probably at Teampull (chapel), about nine miles up Strathnaver from Farr, where he had a cell. He was buried near the cell and the place is marked by a standing stone with a rough cross carved on it. A photo of this stone and more information can be seen on the Highland Pictish Trail website - highlandpictishtrail.co.uk/project/red-priests-stone.

See Towill p. 148; MacQuarrie p. 160; Cat p. 34; Woodside p. 42.

Note: there is a heritage centre in Applecross (opposite Clachan Church) that has information on the saint.

Magnus (d. 1117). Feast day 16th April

Today, the name 'Magnus' is strongly linked to Orkney but this was not so in the years after his death. Orkney was slow to officially recognise Magnus as a saint, possibly due to the embarrassment of his having been killed in a dishonourable manner by his cousin and joint earl, whose family continued as earls of Orkney. However, the ordinary people insisted on his sanctity and attributed many miracles to him, so the process of canonisation began. Over the water in Caithness, there was no such hesitation and he is commemorated at Banniskirk by Watten, Shebster and Spittal, all on routes between mainland Scotland and sea crossings to Orkney. The 'hospital of St Magnus', from which Spittal gets its name, is mentioned in a royal charter in 1476. Banniskirk may be a corruption of his name. His fair was formerly held at Watten-Wester in Caithness around the time of his feast on 16th April, known in the Middle Ages as Magnusmas. There is also a link with Dunbeath as records show that there had been plans to create a trading burgh at Inver called Magnusburgh.[61] There are no other known dedications to Magnus in Scotland. There are a few in England, the main one being at Southwark Bridge, London.[62] He is also remembered in Roskilde, Denmark.

During his life, Magnus Erlendsson was as

---

[61] Crawford p. 224

[62] The auxiliary bishop of Southwark acknowledged this connection by attending the St Magnus 900 celebrations on Orkney in August 2017. He was joined by all the Scottish bishops and those of Oslo and Copenhagen.

much a political figure as a religious one. He held the earldom of Orkney jointly with his cousin, Hakon Paulsson but a rivalry developed between them and Hakon murdered Magnus. The politics of Orkney and Caithness are complex. From the 9th Century, the northern and western islands, with Caithness and Sutherland, were under Viking control. As governance became more organised, each area was ruled by earls. At the beginning of the period in which we are interested, Shetland and Orkney made up one earldom with Caithness with Sutherland another but the earldoms were always kept within the same family to avoid the important waterway, the Pentland Firth, becoming a permanent battleground. Then the King of Norway gained the right to appoint these earls. Then the King of Scotland claimed Caithness and Sutherland, and, eventually, Orkney and Shetland. In the middle of this was the increasing influence of the Church and the local bishops. The process of canonisation of Magnus was under the control of Bishop William of Orkney (1103-1168), who was at first lukewarm but became convinced of the strength of the cause as stories of miracles attributed to Magnus grew. An unusual feature of both the Orkney earldom and church is that both have two saints, as Magnus' nephew, Rognvald, was also canonised (1192), mainly in recognition of his efforts in building the cathedral in honour of his uncle. Both of their relics are within a pillar of the cathedral.

The canonisation process for Magnus has been

studied in detail.[63] The main point of interest to us is that the record of cures attributed to Magnus include far fewer Orkney and Caithness names than Shetland ones. The Shetland people were sufficiently removed from the centre of power of the Earldom that they did not have to worry about the sensibilities of Earl Paul, whose father had murdered Magnus. Archaeologists have identified three chapels on Shetland, the Three Sisters Kirks, that seem to have links with the cathedral in Kirkwall as they are made from the same sandstone and have the same design of piscinas.[64]This raises the question of whether or not these sisters were the three sisters of Magnus.

See Towill p. 155; Cat p. 37, 81; Woodside p. 85; Ecc Hist p. 39, 60; Inv no. 89.

Malie/Mairie (d. 617/618),

Malie is remembered in the church of Kilmalie, formerly the parish church of Golspie, and in a well, *Tobar Malaig* below Melvich, Farr. Malie may be a corruption of Maelrubha or may be Mairie, one of the martyrs of Eigg, as Mairie and Malie are similar in Gaelic. Also *Tobar Malaig* is very similar to Mallaig, the modern port for ferries going to the island of Eigg. The parish of Kilmallie, Inverness-shire, is on the way to Mallaig. In the same area is

---

[63]See Crawford p. 199

[64] A piscina is a stone basin near the altar that drains directly into the ground, allowing the sacred vessels to be rinsed without the water used having to be mixed with other waste water

Glen Mallie, the river Mallie, Invermallie on Loch Arkaig. Other dedications occur in Argylleshire and Fife.

See Cat p. 33; Watson p.290.

Martin (4th century) Feast day11th Nov

There are dedications to Martin of Tours throughout Scotland. A Martin is associated with Donan on Eigg but is not listed as one of the martyrs. The site of St Martin's chapel in an old graveyard to the S of Mains of Ulbster is occupied by a mausoleum, dated 1700. This was the original site of the Ulbster Stone, now in the North Coast Visitors Centre, Thurso. The site at Farr is *Tobar Martain* near Grumbeg burial place.

Martin is linked with Ninian, who is said to have had a devotion to the saint. Modern scholars dismiss the theory that Ninian met Martin while travelling to Rome. There may have been another Martin as the sites at Ulbster and Farr both had carved stones but of different styles.

See Cat p. 37, 81; Ecc Hist p. 39, 60; Inv no. 596. Watson p. 291.

Mary (1st century).

Dedications to Mary, the mother of Jesus, multiplied after the 12th century, sometimes replacing older ones. Kilmory is common but may sometimes be a corruption of e.g. Maelrubha. Sites include the church and well of Crosskirk, Reay (some sources refer to Lybster, Reay which is not to be confused with the village of Lybster on the east coast but refers to the area just south of Crosskirk Bay). This is the oldest ecclesiastical structure in Caithness, dating from the 12th century. Some sources say it was dedicated to St Peter. Close by is St Mary's well. The door of the chapel is similar in structure to chapels at Weir, Linton in Shapinsay, Uyea in Shetland and some early oratories in Ireland. It may have had animal hide curtains. The door is very low. One theory is that this was to ensure that everyone entering the chapel had to bow to the altar before entering. A more practical reason is that it would prevent raiders from storming in. (At the Church of the Nativity in Bethlehem, the door was lowered specifically to prevent men on horseback from entering.)

Other dedications are at Marykirk, John O'Groats; a well and burial place at Scouthal, Watten and at Marykirk of Sibster, Wick on low ground near Wick River and almost opposite where the Burn of Haster joins the Wick river. The Marymas Fair, held in Dunnet in August, suggests a dedication to her in the area.

See Towill p. 170; Cat p. 37; Inv no 39, 55, 338, 594; Ecc Hist p. 39, 55; CFC April '86.

Modan/Medan (c. 6th century). Feast day 14th November

T   here seem to have been two Modans, one associated with Loch Etive, Falkirk and Roseneath and the other being a companion of Drostan in

Caithness. At Freswick, stood St Modan's or Madden's chapel, not far from chapels dedicated to St Drostan at Ackergill and Brabster. Devotional practices linked to St Modan's chapel continued into the 19th century. These have been described as follows:

> even so late as the beginning of the present century devotees were in the habit of resorting to it on Candlemas day and exhibiting proof of the most abject superstition. They first crept round the walls of the chapel on their bare knees, each muttering some petition to the saint, and then going to the neighbouring burn, threw handfuls of water over their heads. After performing this latter part of the ceremony, they adjourned to the nearest ale-house and got drunk![65]

Modan was a common family name of the Earls of Caithness in the 11th century.

See Towill p. 155; Cat p. 37, 81; Woodside p. 33; Ecc Hist p. 49, 333.

Moluag (d. 592). Feast day 25th June

Moluag was a contemporary of Columba. He founded communities on Lismore and Rosemarkie, where he is buried. There are dedications to him throughout the Highlands.

See Towill p. 187, Woodside p. 31; Watson p. 293.

---

[65] Calder's History of Caithness p. 97

Ninian (6th century) feast day 16th Sept

The two sites relevant to our route are burial grounds at Navidale, near Helmsdale (the chapel was burned down in 1544 during clan warfare) with St Ninian's Bay nearby and at Wick.

Ninian is one of the best-known names among the Scottish saints. Traditionally, he was believed to belong to the 4th/5th century, to have travelled to Rome, meeting Martin of Tours on his travels, been ordained a bishop there and returned to Whithorn, to built Candida Casa and found a monastic community.

The latest archaeological evidence suggest that Ninian belongs to the 6th century and was not the original founder of the community at Whithorn. He probably did travel to Rome and build Candida Casa and is certainly the community's most famous member. Dedications to him exist all the way up the east coast, including St Ninian's Isle on Shetland (which had an earlier chapel on the site). The first Abbot of Fearn, Edderton, (d.c.1236) was a canon of Whithorn and may have promoted veneration of Ninian in the north. Watson suggests an interesting theory that devotion to Ninian was encouraged at the time of King David in the 12th C to suggest that the organisational changes being introduced then

> instead of being innovations, were in reality a restoration of the ancient and pure system of Ninian: the monastic Scoto-Irish Church was regarded as an unauthorised and discredited interlude.[66]

---

[66] Watson p.296

Readers will recognise this form of argument from that used by the post-Reformation churches, mentioned earlier.

Rev Scott, mentioned in the Introduction, had a theory that the islands of North and South Ronaldsay, Orkney were dedicated to Ninian. He said that their original name was 'Rinan's-eye' – Ninian's Island. This name was used in some of the sagas. He also quoted evidence of carved crosses in the same style as those at Whithorn, found during the excavation of the Broch of Burrian on North Ronaldsay.

See Towill p. 195; Cat p. 31, 39, 40, 134; MacQuarrie p. 50; Woodside p. 1; Ecc Hist p. 52, 68-73, 334; Watson p. 296.

Peter (1st century). feast day 29th June

Peter was one of Jesus' twelve apostles and the one chosen by him to be the rock on which his Church would be built. Dedications to Peter in the north of Scotland began with Curitan/Boniface (see above) and were often replacements for earlier names. Some sources list the chapel site at Clyne by Brora as one where an earlier dedication was replaced with Peter. Kilphedar on the way to Kildonan is another site that probably had an earlier dedication to one of Donan's followers. On the outskirts of Halkirk, at the left bank of the Olgrinbeg Burn about1/2 mile above its junction with Thurso River, is a chapel site dedicated to Peter (ND 1080 5380). Near-by is a field and hill called 'Appat', suggesting, who was bishop of

Caithness and Sutherland from 1223 to 1245 that the site dates back to the early Celtic saints.

The main site in Caithness is St Peter's Kirk, Thurso. It is supposed to have been founded by Bishop Gilbert, who was bishop of Caithness and Sutherland from 1223 to 1245. The archaeological evidence suggests that some of the structure goes back to the 12th century and various additions and alterations were made as the needs of the community changed over the centuries. The latest changes probably date to just after the Reformation.

There are substantial ruins remaining but these are no longer open to the public as they are in a delicate state, although guided tours can be organised. The impressive gable wall can be seen from the street and is one of the town's best-known landmarks. The west wall has a grave stone dated to the middle of the 14th century.

The kirk was used as a place of worship until 1832, when it was replaced by the present St Peter's and St Andrew's Church of Scotland. For a time, it also served as the local sheriff court and there are records dated 1726 of a vault being utilised as a prison cell.

The original baptismal font is now kept in the North Coast Visitors Centre, near the Kirk.

See Towill p. 218, Cat p. 37, Inv no. 154, 418, 443, Ecc Hist p. 42.

Rectaire/Reet (d. 617/618)

Rectaire, whose name indicates an official, is remembered in Kilreet at Navidale and Helmsdale. He was a disciple of Donan and was martyred with him and his other followers on the Island of Eigg.

See Cat p. 33.

Tarlogan/ Talorcan
(also Talarica, Talorgan, Tarquin, Tarloc, Tarlork, Tarloga, Tarkin)   (7th century) feast day 30th Oct
Here is another name with many variations. It was a common Pictish name. He was a follower of Donan and was with him on Eigg[67]. He is said to have been ordained by Pope Gregory.

In Caithness, Tarlogan is remembered at Tarlogan's Hill (*Torr Tharlogain*) and Tarlogan's Church (*Teampull Tharlogain*), Halkirk where the church dedicated to Fergus now is and at Watten. He founded a chapel at Fordyce in Banffshire, where he is the patron saint. There is a holy well at a burn close to the church, St Tarkin's Well. An annual fair was named for him. He is also associated with Kiltarlity, Inverness-shire, where Beauly Priory is, and a burial ground to the north of Portree, Skye.

See Woodside p. 53; Towill p. 230; Cat p. 35; Ecc Hist p. 9, 59, 80, 334; Watson p. 298.

Thomas a Becket (12th century) Feast day 29th December
Situated about 1/3 mile to the NE of Skinnet Farm and about 4m S of Thurso, are the ruins of the

---

[67] This is disputed by Watson. See p.298 f.1

chapel of St Thomas. This is the original site of the 9th century Skinnet stone, now in the North Coast Visitor Centre (see https://highlandpictishtrail.co.uk/project/north-coast-visitor-centre/ for details). There may have been two ecclesiastical buildings at Skinnet - a church dedicated to St Thomas and an earlier abbey. Gaelic speakers referred to the site as *An Abair*, (Abbey), showing a superseded Celtic foundation. The existing ruins probably date to the late 12th C or very early 13th C as Thomas a'Becket was canonised in 1173. Dedications to him were encouraged by King William (1165 to 1214) who had been a friend of Thomas when the king was in exile in England. When King William founded Arbroath Abbey in 1178, he dedicated it to Thomas. King William had visited Caithness about the turn of the century with an army to avenge the treatment of Bishop John by Earl Harold. So it is possible that the grateful bishop dedicated his new cathedral to the king's favourite saint.

See Cat p. 37; Ecc Hist pp. 42-43, 61; Inv no 91, 445; Towill p. 231; CFC 2006.

Triduana/ (4th or 7th century). Feast day 8th Oct
Also Traddles, Tredwell, Tradwell, Trallew, Trallen, Trollhaena (Norse)

There are legends of Triduana coming from Greece with St Rule/Regulus (4th century) when he brought the relics of St Andrew to Scotland and with St Boniface (8th century). She settled at Rescobie,

Angus. She is associated with Edinburgh and the Highlands. A legend of her plucking out her eyes to repel an unwanted suitor is very similar to that of St Bridget. She is famed for curing eye diseases. She is mentioned in the Orkneyinga Saga (where her name is given as Trollhaena) as curing Bishop John, who had had his eyes plucked out on the orders of Earl Harold of Orkney in 1201 but had them restored when he was taken to her resting place at Ballachly, Achavanich near Loch Stemster[68]. The name 'Achavanich' is translated as 'the monk's field'. Part of the adjoining land was known in ancient times as *Croit Trolla*, the croft of St Triduana. (This resting place would have been the site of a relic, not her grave, which is more likely to be at Restalrig, Edinburgh.) The Restalrig shrine used to be a place of pilgrimage and has recently been restored.

There are also dedications to her at a chapel in Kintradwell (Loth, south of Helmsdale), the House of Peace at Dunbeath (possibly) and St Tredwell's Loch, Papa Westray, Orkney.

See Towill p. 183; Cat p. 36; Woodside p. 60; Ecc Hist p. 63 and 64; Watson p. 334.

This ends the Alphabetical List of Saints.

---

[68]See Crawford p. 251 for details of the story of why Bishop John was attacked.

A Calendar of Saints Days

January 7th	Kentigerna
February 1st	Bridget of Kildare
February 18th	Colman
March 8th	Duthac
March 10th	Kessog
March 16th	Curitan/Boniface
March 20th	Cuthbert
April 1st	Gilbert
April 16th	Magnus
April 21st	Maelrubha
April 23rd	George
April 29th	Catherine of Siena
April 17th	Donan
May 3rd	Fumac
June 9th	Columba
June 25th	Moluag
June 29th	Peter
July 11th	Benedict
July 25th	James the apostle
July 26th	Anne
August 24th	Erchard
August 29th	John the Baptist
September 9th	Ciaran
September 16th	Ninian
September 23rd	Adamnan
October 4th	Francis
October 8th	Triduana
October 13th	Comgan/Cowan
October 30th	Tarlogan
November 11th	Martin

November 13th	Devenic
November 14th	Modan
November 18th	Fergus
November 23rd	Clement
November 25th	Katherine of Alexandria
November 30th	Andrew
December 14th	Drostan
December 27th	John the Apostle
December 29th	Thomas a Becket

BIBLIOGRAPHY

The Holy Bible: Revised Standard Version. Ignatius Press; San Franscisco, 1966.

Beaton, Rev. Donald. *Ecclesiastical History of Caithness and Annals of Caithness Parishes*. Wick: William Rae, 1909.

Caithness Field Club archives at htpps://www.caithness.org. 67; Oct 75; 76; 82; 83; 85; 86; 87; 89; 2001; 2006.

Calder, J.T. *History of Caithness from the Tenth Century*. Wick: William Rae, 1887. Re-published 1973 by Stansfield, Fortrose.

J.B. Craven, ven. D.D. *Journals of Bishop Forbes*. London: Skeffington & Son, Ltd., 1886.

Light of the North Aberdeen Diocesan magazine
Issue no 5 on Drostan: Issue no 6 on Devenic; Issue no 7 on Duthac; Issue no 8 on Fergus; Issue no.20 on Drostan.

Farmer, D. *Oxford Dictionary of Saints*. Oxford: O.U.P., 1997.

Haldane, A.R.B. *The Drove Roads of Scotland*. Edinburgh: Birlinn Ltd., 1997.

MacGregor, R. *Hills of the North Rejoice!* available online from curlewcottage.com.

MacKay, A. and Beaton, D. *The History of the Province of Cat (Caithness and Sutherland), From the Earliest Times to the Year 1615*. Wick: Peter Reid & Coy., Ltd, 1914. Reproduced by Leopold Classic Library and available at http://tinyurl.com/leopold-historyofprovinc00mackuoft.

MacQuarrie, A. *The Saints of Scotland: Essays in Scottish*

Church History AD 450-1093. Edinburgh: John Donald Publishers Ltd, 1997.

Reith, M. *God in Our Midst: Prayers and Devotions from the Celtic Tradition*. London: Triangle/SPCK, 1975.

Scott, Rev Dr A.B. *St Donnan the Great and his Muinntir'* from The Transactions of the Scottish Ecclesiological Society Vol I, part iii 1906.

Chapters in the History of the Church of the Picts (II) – S. Finbarr of Caithness and Ulster in Transactions of the Gaelic Society of Inverness 6.2.1908.

S. Drostan of Buchan and Caithness in Transactions of the Gaelic Society of Inverness1.4.1909.

Sinclair, A. *Memories of the Causeymire*. North of Scotland Newspapers Ltd, 1988.

Strange Tales of the Causeymire. North of Scotland Newspapers Ltd, 1988.

The Royal Commission on the Ancient and Historical Monuments and Constructions of Scotland. *Third Report and Inventory of Monuments and Constructions in the County of Caithness*. London: His Majesty's Stationary Office, 1911.

Towill, E. S. *Saints of Scotland*. Edinburgh: Saint Andrew Press.1983.

Watson, W.J. *The Celtic Place-Names of Scotland*. Edinburgh: Birlinn Limited, 2004.

Woodside, J. *Together in Christ: Following the Northern Saints*. R.C. Diocese of Aberdeen, 2016.

Some Background Reading

If anyone is interested in modern scholarship surrounding the Celtic Church, there is much to choose from. To get an introduction, try:
Olsen, Ted. *Christianity and the Celts*. Downer's Grove, Il: InterVarsity Press, 2003.

For a more detailed approach, giving opposing views on the Celtic v Roman argument, the best-known writer in the field is Ian Bradley, who writes from the point of view of the Celtic Church as a separate organisation from the Roman Church. His university colleague, Donald Meek takes the opposite view and Tom Clancy acts as a referee between them!

Ian Bradley *The Celtic Way*. Darton, Longman and Todd, London, 1993.

Donald E Meek *The Quest for Celtic Christianity*. The Handsel Press Ltd, Edinburgh, 2000.

Proff T.O. Clancy *Celtic or Catholic – Writing the history of Scottish Christianity, A.D. 664-1093*. 2002 and available at https://archive.org.

About the author: I am a founder member of the Northern Saints Trails Group SCIO and the Northern Pilgrims' Way Group SCIO. Now living in Caithness surrounded by children and grandchildren, I was brought up in Moidart on the West coast of Scotland on a small croft where the living conditions were not so very far removed from those of the Celtic saints mentioned in this book.

Traditional Hay-making

This shows the author in 1972 on the family croft. The small mounds were covered with hessian sacking rather than thatch. The larger structures, a comparatively modern invention, consisted of four poles with rope wound round them. The hay was partially dried in the mounds then draped over the larger structures. As these were hollow, they allowed for better drying. The end result was stored in barns.

Printed in Great Britain
by Amazon

84253544R00129